WISDOM AND ✱ KNOWLE
✱ ✱ SHALL BE THE ✱
STABILITY OF THY TIM

RETRO NY

RETRO NY

A Guide to Rediscovering Old New York

Chuck Lawliss

Taylor Trade Publishing
Dallas, Texas

Designed by Janis Owens

Photo on pg. i by Janis Owens
All other photography by Joe DiMaggio and JoAnne Kalish

Published by Taylor Publishing Company
1550 West Mockingbird Lane
Dallas, Texas 75235
www.taylorpub.com

Library of Congress Cataloging-in-Publication Data
Lawliss, Chuck.
  Retro NY : a guide to rediscovering old New York / Chuck Lawliss.
    p. cm.
  Includes index.
  ISBN 0-87833-171-9
    1. New York (N.Y.)—Guidebooks. 2. Historic sites—New York (State)—
New York—Guidebooks. 3. New York (N.Y.)—Buildings, structures, etc.—Guidebooks.
I. Title: Retro New York. II. Title.
F128.18.L346 2000
917.47'10443—dc21   00-022185

10 9 8 7 6 5 4 3 2 1

Printed in the United States of America

Contents

INTRODUCTION: EVERYTHING OLD IS NEW AGAIN

If you've known New York for a long time, your memory has fashioned your own special New York. It selects your favorite period, polishes the good things, tones down the bad. The sun is shining and you're young and happy and in love. It makes the New York of today look pretty grim, like something out of Chaplin's *Modern Times*, except you can see much humor in it.

If you're new to New York, another trap awaits. If you don't take time to learn about the city and experience its time-tested pleasures, you'll miss out on one of the world's great pleasures. Sadly, a lot of people do miss out. To paraphrase Mae West, "New York is a banquet and most of the suckers in it are starving to death."

This book was written to help you experience the pleasures of the past, whether for the first time or for the first time in a long time. Specifically, it's about how and where to find these pleasures, either in their original form or reconfigured into a new form. These are retro pleasures; hence the title—*Retro NY*.

New York is forever shifting and changing like a kaleidoscope. Turn your back on it for a minute, in fact, and something is sure to happen. To stay away for a couple of weeks is to come back feeling out of sync, a regular hick. Sometimes a brief weekend is all it takes.

The city always seems to be sorting itself out, or reinventing itself. Old buildings disappear; new buildings appear. Old restaurants close and new ones open. Turn around twice and all the great nightclubs are gone—El Morocco, the Copa, the Stork Club. To stay in tune with New York, we must be adaptable. For what New York gives in return, it is a small price to pay.

I grew up in a village in Vermont and fell in love with New York when I visited it with my parents. I was 12 years old and hopelessly impressionable. We went to Radio City Music Hall, Chinatown—the things that first-time-in-the-big-city tourists do. Later I would live and work in New York for 35 years. I had the honor to work for my favorite newspaper, the *New York Herald Tribune*, and I would still be happily there if it hadn't died in the 1960s.

When I arrived in New York there were fights nearly every Friday night in Madison Square Garden. There were three big-league baseball teams in town. There were two big-league hockey teams; there was racing at four thoroughbred tracks by day and two big harness tracks at night. There was international polo on Long Island; there was international tennis at Forest Hills. There never was a day when sports weren't big in New York, bigger than in any other city.

Broadway was in its glory. My first year in the city I worked on a story titled "Broadway: The Best Season Ever." It was the season of Ingrid Bergman's *Saint Joan*, Susan Strasburg's *The Diary of Anne Frank*, and the musicals *Damn Yankees*, *The Most Happy Fellow*, and *My Fair Lady*. But theater memories would fill a book of their own.

Remember Toots Shor's old restaurant on 51st across from the Music Hall? That's where the ballplayers hung out. "21" was around the corner on 52nd Street. That's where millionaires hung out. And the great restaurants: Le Pavillon, The Colony, Quo Vadis, The Gloucester House, The Press Box, La Fonda del Sol in the Time-Life Building.

All of which proves nothing more than that I loved New York in those years. And I love New York now. I miss some of the old things; I like some of the new things. I'm happy with my memories; I'm happy with the New York I'm in now. Perhaps my suggestions will help you enjoy the old and the new with equal gusto.

Lower Manhattan

More than two hundred years ago, Samuel Johnson said, "When a man is tired of London, he is tired of life, for there is in London all that life can afford." A pity Mr. Johnson didn't make it to New York in the twenty-first century. It would *really* have blown him away!

ALL AROUND THE TOWN

Exploring the Neighborhoods

Most New Yorkers straddle two neighborhoods, the one where they live and the one where they work. The city's other neighborhoods are *terra incognita*, as unfamiliar as Tacoma or Biloxi. This is a pity because all the city's neighborhoods are distinctly different, have a rich history, and reward the curious visitor. Explore the neighborhoods; it will give you a new perspective on the city. And it's fun. Here are bits of history to help you on your way.

Lower Manhattan The city's oldest and most historic neighborhood is the area from the Hudson to the East River below Chambers Street. This is where, in 1625, the Dutch built Fort Amsterdam to protect their little settlement, Nieuw Amsterdam. The British finally took Manhattan away from the Dutch in 1674. It was a cosmopolitan settlement; as early as 1664 a priest recorded 18 languages spoken in the colony.

The British found New Yorkers unruly and hard to govern. In 1734 John Peter Zenger, a printer, was jailed for "seditious libel" for having criticized British officials. He won the case, though, establishing the principle of a free press in the process. The city was active in the events leading up to the American Revolution and staged its own Tea Party in 1774. On July 9, 1776, rioters toppled the statue of George III in Bowling Green and melted it down into bullets.

After the war, Washington said good-bye to his officers at Fraunces Tavern at the corner of Pearl and Broad Streets and later took the presidential oath on the balcony of Federal Hall on Wall Street, where a larger-than-life statue of him now stands. For the next year New York was the capital of the United States.

By 1810, when City Hall was being built on the city green, the north side of the building was covered with common brownstone, because no one thought City Hall would be viewed from that side. But by the end of the decade New York had expanded another ten to fifteen blocks, and by 1850 it had pushed two miles to 14th Street.

It soon became a tradition for the mayor to greet distinguished visitors on the steps of City Hall.

The towering skyscrapers of Lower Manhattan

Horace Greeley, Ulysses S. Grant, and Abraham Lincoln all lay in state in the rotunda, and some 60,000 people followed Lincoln's coffin up Broadway.

A 1735 fire destroyed much of Lower Manhattan, but it made a speedy recovery and by the end of the War of 1812 it was the leading port and commercial center in the country. Insurance companies, merchants, lawyers, and financiers were crowding out families in the area that became the Financial District.

Today a visitor to Lower Manhattan can see only a few of the old buildings: Federal Hall, the Customs House on Bowling Green, Trinity Church, and St. Paul's Chapel. In the park at the foot of Broadway is an oval area, all that remains of Bowling Green, which started as a Dutch cattle market.

South Street Seaport Museum

Many of the early nineteenth century buildings in the area around Fulton Street at the East River have been preserved as a reminder of the days when this was called the "Street of Ships." Three historic ships are on display: the square-rigger *Wavetree*, the four-masted bark *Peking*, and the *Ambrose Lightship*. Of particular

The South Street Seaport, with Manhattan looming in the background

interest is Schermerhorn Row (Fulton between Front and South Streets), twenty-two blocks filled with Greek Revival, Georgian, Federal, and Victorian warehouses and store buildings dating from 1811.
Museum information:
☎ 212/669-9400.

Chinatown Chinese started to settle here in the mid-1800s as racial problems on the West Coast drove them east. The first Chinese here were attracted to the laundry and restaurant businesses. Self-help associations called tongs developed into underworld gangs, and the "tong wars" hurt the reputation of Chinatown. The tongs are now merchants' associations and Chinatown is considered one of the city's most stable areas. **The Chinese Museum** (8 Pell Street, 212/964-1542) displays artifacts of the community's early days. Originally Chinatown was an eight-block area bounded by the Bowery and Mulberry, Worth, and Canal Streets, but it has expanded over the years.

Little Italy During the peak of Italian immigration, from 1880 to

1915, the area around Mulberry Street became known as Little Italy, and many of the tenement buildings date from that period. Over the years many residents have moved on, and Little Italy has lost territory to Chinatown. It still thrives, however, and seems to have as many Italian restaurants as Chinatown has Chinese restaurants. The 1909 police headquarters at 240 Centre Street, the 1816 Stephen van Rensselaer House at 140 Mulberry Street, once the governor's city dwelling, and St. Patrick's Old Cathedral at 260 Mulberry Street are all worth a visit.

Lower East Side The swampy area northeast of the new City Hall was thought worthless, but when waves of immigrants began arriving, real-estate developers began building tenements, rental buildings that produced the most money from the space. The Irish came first, arriving in the 1840s. Between 1881 and 1910, 1.5 million Jews fled Eastern Europe, creating the largest Jewish settlement in the world on the Lower East Side. The area became a slum—poor, overcrowded, filled with sweatshops and suffering.

Somehow the area was able to support a rich intellectual life. Yiddish theater thrived on the

Celebrating the Chinese New Year in New York's Chinatown

Bowery, and publications included Emma Goldman's *Mother Earth* and the Yiddish-language *Jewish Daily Forward.* Labor leader Samuel Gompers was born here, and many artists who would become famous studied at the Educational Alliance.

The Bowery began as the Bowerie, a dirt road leading to Peter Stuyvesant's farm, or *"bouwerie."* During the American Revolution it became an evacuation route for Washington's troops. In the early 1800s, the Bowery became first an affluent residential area then a theater district. Decline set in during the 1870s and the Bowery became the city's skid row. During the Depression it attracted the unemployed and dispossessed. The Henry Street Settlement Houses (263, 265, and 267 Henry Street) are typical Greek Revival residences. The Settlement, founded in 1893, was one of the first social service organizations in the country, and is still active in the neighborhood. The Lower East Side is bounded by the East River and Lafayette, Chambers, and Houston Streets.

SoHo and TriBeCa These are new names for old parts of the city. SoHo was coined to describe the district south of Houston Street; TriBeCa the wedge-shaped "Triangle Below Canal Street," which includes the area bounded by Lafayette Street, the Hudson, and Chambers and Houston Streets. In the seventeenth century, farms and estates filled this area. Houses started going up in the early 1800s, and from 1840 to 1860 this was the center of the city, complete with department stores and hotels.

As the city continued to expand to the north, SoHo filled with businesses in prefabricated cast-iron buildings. The so-called "King of Greene Street" (number 72–76) and "Queen of Greene Street" (number 28–30) are notable examples of cast-iron architecture. In 1970 the city permitted artists to move into the empty cast-iron buildings, legalizing a movement that had been going on for a decade. Then came galleries, boutiques, and nouvelle cuisine restaurants. SoHo now is a historic district.

TriBeCa retains its bohemian character. Because it is near the City Hall area, which has a large daytime working population, it has resisted the tide of fad enterprises, and hasn't been overwhelmed like SoHo.

Astor Place District Sometimes called the East Village, this architecturally diverse area lies between 14th and Houston Streets, Broadway and the East River. Once it was all part of the farm of Peter Stuyvesant, and its most notable structure, St. Mark's Church-in-the-Bowery (Second Avenue and 10th Street), is believed to have been built on the site of Stuyvesant's own chapel. In the 1830s the area was home to some of the city's finest families, including Astors, Delanos, and Vanderbilts.

The Cooper Union Foundation Building (East 7th Street between

Cooper Square and Third Avenue) was built in 1859 to provide a free education for deserving youths of both sexes. Philanthropist Peter Cooper was an industrialist and inventor. He built the country's first locomotive, Tom Thumb.

The only surviving examples of the residential architecture in the area are on Colonnade Row (428–434 Lafayette Street). Four of the original nine townhouses remain. Built in 1833, they were once owned by such prominent people as Warren Delano, grandfather of Franklin Delano Roosevelt.

On the southern edge of the district is the fanciful 1885 Puck Building (295–309 Lafayette Street). A restored Romanesque Revival building, it was the home of the humor magazine *Puck,* and a statue of the mischievous sprite is over the main entrance.

Greenwich Village This was originally a village cut off from the rest of the city by its location and preference of its residents. Much of Greenwich Village still has tree-lined, winding streets and low-rise buildings. It has an atmosphere of unconventionality and a lively street life.

When the Dutch arrived, this was the site of an Indian village called Sapokanican. Then came large landowners like Admiral Peter Warren and the De Lancey family. When epidemics of smallpox, cholera, and yellow fever ravaged the city from the 1790s to the early 1800s, New Yorkers settled in Greenwich Village, which was far from the congested city. In the

1830s, prominent families began building town houses at Washington Square, which had become a park. Society also took over Fifth Avenue. This state of affairs didn't last long, however. The rich moved on to Gramercy Park, Madison Square, and upper Fifth Avenue, and by 1860, the Village was a quiet, middle-class area.

When the rich left, some of their houses were divided into flats and studios, and artists and writers moved in. Former Villagers included Edgar Allan Poe, Horace Greeley, Walt Whitman, and Mark Twain. Edna St. Vincent Millay once lived in the narrowest house in the city, at 75½ Bedford Street. By the beginning of World War I, the Village became the seat of American bohemia. The Village for years has been identified with radical movements in politics and the arts.

The narrow, twisting streets of the Village have rich historical associations. Theodore Dreiser and Sherwood Anderson were neighbors on St. Luke's Place. Poet e. e. cummings lived in the tiny mews called Patchin Place. Edgar Allan Poe once lived in a house that still stands at 45 West 3rd Street and in 1845 was treated for a cold at the Northern Dispensary (Waverly Place and Christopher Place). More recently, Dylan Thomas frequented the White Horse Tavern (567 Hudson Street) and died in a Village hospital after one of his famous binges there.

Historic Greenwich Village

Washington Square In the early days this area was used at one time or another as a parade ground, a hanging ground, and a potter's field. Washington Square Park was laid out in 1827 and soon elegant homes were being built on its borders. The Greek Revival houses along Washington Square North called The Row were built between 1831 and 1833. Edith Wharton, William Dean Howells, John Dos Passos, and Eleanor Roosevelt were among the celebrities who lived here at various times.

In 1889 a wooden arch was erected in the park at the foot of Fifth Avenue to commemorate the centennial of the inauguration of George Washington. The residents of the area liked it so well that they commissioned Stanford White to design the present Washington Arch, built of marble and dedicated in 1895.

Nearby is New York University. Albert Gallatin, Thomas Jefferson's secretary of the treasury, and other prominent New Yorkers founded the institution in 1831 as a nonsectarian alternative to Episcopalian Columbia University. It is now the largest private university in the country. NYU's Brown Building on Washington Place once was a factory in which fire killed 146 workers, many of them young immigrant girls, of the Triangle Shirtwaist Company in 1911.

Chelsea Clement Clarke Moore, distinguished Hebrew scholar and developer of Chelsea, is best remembered for his beloved poem, *A Visit from St. Nicholas*. After inheriting the land from his grandfather, he laid out residential streets with houses set back 10 feet, banned manufacturing from the area, and donated an entire block to the General Theological Seminary, where he was on the faculty. Chelsea borders are somewhat vague. The area is bounded by West 19th to about 29th Street and from Eighth Avenue to the Hudson River.

The country's motion picture industry started in Chelsea in 1905 and flourished for a decade. Adolph Zukor's Famous Players Studio, which employed Mary Pickford and John Barrymore, produced films here. The Astoria Studios in Queens, however, built a bigger facility, and eventually Hollywood beckoned and the movie business moved on.

In the 1950s and 1960s, urban renewal replaced slums with housing projects, and Federal and Greek Revival town houses were restored. The Chelsea Hotel, on West 23rd Street, is a reminder of Chelsea's theater days, when actors and playwrights stayed there.

Ladies' Mile During the Gilded Age in the 1890s, the city's most fashionable restaurants, hotels, theaters, shops, department stores, and office buildings were from 8th to 23rd Street along Broadway and adjacent Fifth and Sixth Avenues. W. and J. Sloane and Arnold Constable built monumental emporiums on Broadway. R. H. Macy opened a store on 14th Street, and B. Altman opened one on Sixth Avenue. These stores were designed by the most prominent architects of the day.

This grand era lasted until 1914 when Lord & Taylor left its extravagant Second Empire-style building at 801 Broadway at 21st Street and moved north to its present location at Fifth Avenue and 38th Street. Other establishments followed, until Ladies' Mile became a district of architectural classics forgotten by the rest of the city.

Union Square Just off Ladies' Mile is Union Square, a park bounded by Broadway, Park Avenue South, 14th Street, and 17th Street. It was laid out in 1831 by Samuel B. Ruggles, who also designed nearby Gramercy Park. After fashionable New York moved uptown, the park became a center for political protest and demonstrations. It contains some of the best statuary in the city. Among them are Henry Kirke Brown's equestrian statue of *George Washington* (1856) and a statue of the *Marquis de Lafayette*, by Auguste Bartholdi, sculptor of the Statue of Liberty (1876).

At the triangle formed where Broadway crosses Fifth Avenue at 23rd Street stands the famous Flatiron Building, the head of Ladies' Mile. The ornate, intricately detailed structure, designed by D. H. Burnham, was the world's tallest building (300 feet) when completed in 1902.

Madison Square Park, which is north of 23rd Street, also contains one of the best statues in the city, the 1881 *Admiral Farragut Monument* by Augustus Saint-Gaudens. The base was designed by the leading architect of his time, Stanford White. White's handsome Madison Square Garden, topped by a controversial nude statue of the goddess Diana by Saint-Gaudens, stood from 1890 to 1925 on the east side of the park. White was shot to death in 1906 in the building's roof garden by a jealous husband, Harry K. Thaw. It was one of the most sensational crimes of the century.

Gramercy Park In 1831 Samuel B. Ruggles, a real-estate developer, laid out sixty-six building lots around the only private residential park in the city. He named the street running north from the park Lexington Avenue and the street going south Irving Place, after his friend Washington Irving. The park is restricted to area residents who pay a maintenance fee. The only time its sanctity has been violated was when troops camped there during the Civil War draft riots.

In the park is a statue of the actor Edwin Booth dressed as Hamlet. Booth purchased the 1845 town house at 15 Gramercy Park South and had Stanford White remodel it in 1888 as a club for actors called The Players. Next door is the National Arts Club. Built in 1845, it was purchased and remodeled in 1874 by Samuel J. Tilden, a New York governor and the unsuccessful candidate for president in 1876. South of the park at 66 Irving Place is Pete's Tavern, one of the oldest taverns in the city. William Sydney Porter (O. Henry)

The famous wedge of the Flatiron Building

wrote his famous short story "The Gift of the Magi" in the second booth on the right. Gramercy Park is bounded by 23rd and 18th Streets, Third and Park Avenues.

Murray Hill Today this is a mostly commercial area with brownstone residences on the tree-lined cross streets. It extends from Lexington to Fifth Avenue and from 34th to 42nd Streets. For a time in the mid-1800s, however, Murray Hill was home to many of the city's wealthiest and most socially prominent families. A reminder of this period is the home and library of the financier J. P. Morgan, at 231 Madison Avenue. Another landmark is the former Advertising Club at 23 Park Avenue, a Renaissance palazzo designed by McKim, Mead & White for J. Hampton Robb.

Kips Bay North and east of Gramercy Park is an area named after the farm established there by Jacobus Kip in 1655. The area bounded by 32rd and 38th Streets is called Kips Bay.

By the late 1890s, when J. P. Morgan moved to Murray Hill, a gentlemen's agreement restricted the streets of Murray Hill to private houses. Until the invasion of high-rise hotels and apartments in the 1920s, it was a neighborhood of elegant mansions, many of which still stand.

Garment Center and Theater District
The fashion and theater districts fit together in a relatively small area of the city—West 34th to West 59th Streets, from Sixth Avenue to the Hudson. Before 1900, the garment trade was on the Lower East Side, but by 1915 it had moved north along Broadway and Sixth Avenue as far as West 30th Street, replacing part of the tough Tenderloin District. However, the garment workers soon were getting too close to fashionable Fifth Avenue, and two garment workshop buildings were built at Seventh Avenue and West 37th Street, a comfortable distance away.

The theaters also followed the city as it surged north. The Metropolitan opened at West 39th Street and Broadway in 1883, and the Floradora Girls were already performing across the street at the Casino Theater. Soon, though, theaters were being crowded out by new retail stores. When Macy's built at West 34th and Broadway, it replaced, among other structures, Koster & Bial's Music Hall. In the early 1900s theaters were built north of West 42nd Street, and the owners formed a syndicate, forcing the downtown theaters out of business. The syndicate's power increased in 1916, when the Shubert brothers began to build new theaters in the Times Square area, which the subways had put within easy reach of the entire city. Other entrepreneurs followed, and the theater district has been defined ever since as the area bounded by West 42nd Street, West 52nd Street, Broadway, and Ninth Avenue.

Fifth Avenue The rich began to move to Fifth in 1837. Railroad

Macy's department store

tycoon Jay Gould built a mansion
at 47th and Fifth, and began entertaining important friends like
Russell Sage and William H.
Vanderbilt. By the late 1890s,
Vanderbilt had built three mansions on the west side of Fifth
Avenue at 51st Street. His son,
William K. Vanderbilt, built a
palace of his own a few doors
uptown. Another Vanderbilt,
Cornelius II, built an even grander
mansion at 58th Street.

Fifth Avenue now extends from
Washington Square to 138th Street,
but it's the midtown section,
anchored by Rockefeller Center
and St. Patrick's Cathedral, that
epitomizes the city in the minds of
most people. Until the end of the
nineteenth century, Fifth Avenue
was largely residential. The arrival
of B. Altman's department store at
34th Street and Lord & Taylor at
38th Street was the beginning of
the end of the residential era.

The Astors also made their mark
on Fifth Avenue. When William
Waldorf Astor built the Waldorf
hotel next to his aunt's mansion on
Fifth Avenue and West 33rd Street,
she retaliated by tearing down her
house and building a hotel, the
Astoria. Then she built a
Renaissance palazzo for herself on
"Millionaire's Row," as Fifth
Avenue was called. Both hotels
were later destroyed to make room
for the Empire State Building, and
the Waldorf-Astoria reopened in its
present site at Park Avenue and
East 49th Street. Today only a few
reminders of the old mansions
remain on Fifth Avenue, including

Rockefeller Plaza

the two that house Cartier and Versace at East 52nd Street.

Turtle Bay The land around Turtle Bay, now the East Forties, once belonged to Admiral Peter Warren of the British navy, who had married into the fashionable De Lancey family. Just before the American Revolution, the Sons of Liberty raided the military armaments and munitions stored on the Warren farm and sailed them to Boston. Horace Greeley and Edgar Allan Poe once lived in Turtle Bay, which now is dominated by the United Nations headquarters.

The Upper East Side Until after the Civil War, this area, from 57th to 96th Streets, was where the fashionable came to escape the heat of summer. At the end of the nineteenth century, a necklace of mansions followed the shore of the East River north to Harlem. The Boston Post Road, now Third Avenue, made access to the city below Canal Street convenient, and summer residents who were unhurried traveled by steamboat. By 1870 the old summer houses had been converted to year-round use. A few years later the coming of elevated railroads on Second and Third Avenues opened the area to the working class.

Most of the great buildings were built between 1900 and 1920. The original owners were fine families who moved here from downtown. The western part of the area, except for the German village of Yorkville, was all open country. When work started on Central Park

in 1857, there were farms here. Steam trains along Park Avenue made this an undesirable residential neighborhood. It wasn't until 1913, when the New York Central electrified its trains and covered the Park Avenue tracks, that the Upper East Side became a desirable place for the rich to live.

Yorkville First settled by wealthy German farmers and estate owners in the late 1700s, Yorkville was later taken over by German immigrants and became a thriving working-class neighborhood until the Third Avenue Elevated was torn down and the high-rise apartments began to go up. The main thoroughfare was East 86th Street from Third Avenue to the East River. At the north end of Carl Schurz Park on Yorkville's eastern edge is Gracie Mansion, the official residence of the mayor of New York since Fiorello La Guardia in 1942. Built in 1799 as the country home of the merchant Archibald Gracie, the elegant villa is surrounded by a fence and trees and is open to the public by appointment (212/570-4741).

Museum Mile begins at the Metropolitan Museum of Art on the park side of Fifth Avenue and East 82nd Street and ends with the Museum of the City of New York at 103rd Street. In between are the International Center of Photography, the Cooper-Hewitt National Design Museum, the Solomon R. Guggenheim Museum, and the Jewish Museum.

Madison Avenue has been a street of mostly art galleries,

O L O M O N   R   G U G G E N H E I M   M U S E U

The Solomon R. Guggenheim Museum

jewelry stores, antique shops, clothing boutiques, and restaurants. Park Avenue, with its landscaped center island, is lined by dignified apartment houses and old mansions, many of which are now foreign missions or clubs. Lexington Avenue is a downscale Madison Avenue. A small neighborhood around Madison in the East Nineties called Carnegie Hill is home to many young couples opting to raise families in the city. Third, Second, and First Avenues are lined with restaurants, singles bars, and shops. On the side streets are tenements and modest town houses.

West Side Washington Irving described this area as a "sweet rural valley," but today it is as diverse and densely populated as any area in the city. First settled by Eastern European Jews and other immigrants from the Lower East Side, the West Side has always been more independent and laidback than the East Side.

The West Side is a vibrant neighborhood, bounded by Central Park West, the Hudson, West 59th, and West 86th Streets. Near Central

Park are sidewalk cafes, in-line skaters zipping by, young mothers with carriages, and well-dressed crowds pouring in and out of Lincoln Center. Riverside Drive, at the neighborhood's western edge, once was a street of upper-middle-class town houses with spectacular river views. It had a few mansions, like the one Charles Schwab built in 1906 at West 73rd Street. Many private homes were replaced in the 1920s by apartment buildings.

West Siders believe that Central Park West, the neighborhood's eastern edge, is classier than Fifth Avenue. The buildings are more distinguished, they say, and the street wider. Most of the buildings were built as apartments rather than houses, including the Dakota, the city's first luxury apartment house. Twin-towered art-deco apartment buildings like the San Remo and the Eldorado make Central Park West's skyline unique.

West End Avenue, once lined with Queen Anne-style and Romanesque row houses, was supposed to be the West Side's commercial street, and Broadway was to be the residential area, which accounts for its generous width and the mall in the center. But it worked out the other way around: Broadway became commercial; West End Avenue, residential.

Upper West Side This neighborhood, bounded by Central Park, the Hudson, West 86th Street, and Cathedral Parkway/West 110th Street, is going through the same gentrification process that has changed the character of the Lower West Side over the past 30 years. The commercial area is pushing north along Broadway and along Columbus and Amsterdam Avenues, and the residential area is pushing south between Columbus and Central Park West.

The West Side north of West 86th Street, which recently was a dilapidated Old-Worldish area, now has high-rise apartment buildings, attractive retail stores, and attractive restaurants. The amenities here include easy access to Central Park and Riverside Park, a 50-block oasis along the Hudson.

At 122nd Street and Riverside Drive is the General Grant National Memorial, known more popularly as Grant's Tomb. The Civil War general and president is entombed in an imposing granite tomb with his wife, Julia Dent Grant. The interior is a copy of Napoleon's tomb in Paris. 212/666-1640.

⚜

Up in Central Park: An Explorer's Guide

Central Park is the largest open space in Manhattan, and it's one of the greatest parks in the world. More than 15 million people wander through the park every year. Some 250 species of birds are regularly sighted in its treetops, and its 843 acres are completely man-made. In fact, Central Park is such an integral part of the city that we forget the slow painful process that brought it into being.

It began in 1844, when William Cullen Bryant, poet, nature lover, and newspaper editor, persuaded the city to acquire the tract for $5 million, a price many considered outrageous. The land was swampy and occupied by squatters' shanties. Fourteen years later, Frederick Law Olmsted, a journalist who would become the country's first professional landscape architect, and his partner Calvert Vaux submitted the winning design for the park. It envisioned the park as a "democratic development of the highest significance," and insisted that it be open to all, which many parks weren't at the time.

Construction of the park lasted twenty years, involving thousands of workmen and a half-million cubic feet of topsoil that had to be carted in. Central Park finally opened to the public in the winter of 1859.

The park is bounded by Central Park South, 110th Street, Central Park West, and Fifth Avenue. It can be entered through eighteen gates; a winding road runs around the entire park, while sunken crossroads unobtrusively carry traffic across. In the park are seemingly endless paths, a wildlife conservatory, playgrounds, a bridle trail, two skating rinks, a zoo and a children's zoo, a carousel, two lakes and two ponds, several cafes, two forts, a band shell, a chess and checkers house, boat rentals, an open-air theater, and an amazing number of statues.

Central Park is sufficiently large and diverse to deserve a guidebook all its own, but here are a few time-tested pleasures:

A quick way to shed your cares for an hour or so is to rent a boat at the **Loeb Boathouse** and explore **The Lake**. The boathouse is open from 10 A.M. to 6 P.M. Monday–Friday, 11:30–6 Saturday–Sunday. **74th Street at the East Drive** ☎ **212/517-2233**

Watch lawn bowling or croquet at the manicured **Bowling Green** at **70th Street and the West Drive**. You can get a permit to play by phoning ☎ **212/350-8133**. Beware: Players take their game very seriously.

Say hello to some of the 450 animals who make their home at **The Zoo**, near the southeast corner of the park from 63rd to 65th Streets. Redesigned and rebuilt in 1988, the zoo provides more natural homes for bears and sea lions, and two flocks of penguins play under a simulated ice pack in a pool with glass walls. Monkeys swing in trees

Finding Where You Are in the Park

If you're not sure where you are in Central Park, find the nearest lamppost. The first two numbers on the post signify the nearest numbered east-west street.

A bird's-eye view of Central Park

One of the inhabitants of the Central Park Zoo

in a mock-African environment. The 5½-acre complex is administrated by the New York Zoological Society. The cafeteria, shop, and gallery at the southern edge are accessible without entering the grounds. Admission: $3.50 for adults, $1.50 for students and seniors, $.50 for children 3 to 12. Open 10–5 Monday–Friday, 10:30–5:30 weekends. ☎ 212/861-6030

Enjoy a production at the 2,000-seat open-air **Delacorte Theatre**, the home of Shakespeare in the Park. Free performances are given Tuesday–Sunday evenings at 8 from late June through early September.

Tickets are distributed, one per person in line, beginning at 6:15, or at the Public Theater, 425 Lafayette Street, on the day of performance. **80th Street at West Drive** ☎ 212/861-PAPP

Pay your respects to the memory of John Lennon at the memorial grove in **Strawberry Fields,** rehabilitated and maintained with funds provided by his widow, Yoko Ono. The former Beatle was assassinated in 1980 in front of the entrance to the Dakota, the apartment house in which he lived. The Dakota overlooks this tranquil spot. **72nd Street at Central Park West**

Free Tours of the Park

The Central Park Conservatory sponsors free tours of the park. For details, phone 212/772-0210

Spend a winter afternoon showing off your double axels at the **Wollman Memorial Skating Rink.** Admission: $4 for adults, $3 for children under 12. Skate rental $6. Open 10 A.M. to 6 P.M. Tuesday–Friday, 11–8 Saturday–Sunday. Ice-skating early September through late April, roller-skating at other times. **59th Street at Sixth Avenue** ☎ **212/396-1010**

Savor the magnificent view at **The Pond**, a crescent-shaped haven for ducks. From the bridge at the northern end you'll see The Plaza Hotel reflected in the water. Be sure to bring your camera. **60th to 67th Streets at Fifth Avenue**

Ride one of the fifty-eight hand-carved wooden horses on **The Carousel**, built in 1908 and brought here from Coney Island in 1951. Open weekdays 10 A.M. to 6 P.M., weekends to 5:30, weather permitting. Admission: $1 per ride or $5 for six rides (all ages). **65th Street at Center Drive** ☎ **212/879-0244**

Attend a concert on **The Great Lawn**, where a half-million people listened to Simon & Garfunkel in 1981. Besides pop performers, the New York Philharmonic and the Metropolitan Opera give several free performances here each summer, usually attracting about 100,000 people. Come early and picnic while you wait. During the early years of the Depression, these 15 acres were filled with squatters' shacks known as a "Hooverville." **80th to 85th Streets between the East–West Drives**

The Heights North of West 110th Street, the land becomes hilly, and geography defines neighborhood boundaries all the way to Spuyten Duyvil, where the Hudson meets the East River. Morningside Heights is dominated by educational institutions—Columbia University, Barnard College, Union Theological Seminary, and the Jewish Theological Seminary. Also in the neighborhood is the Cathedral Church of St. John the Divine, Riverside Church, and, on a hill overlooking the Hudson, Grant's Tomb.

From West 125th Street to West 153rd Street is Hamilton Heights, named for Alexander Hamilton, who had a country estate there. The area was undeveloped until after 1904, when the subway came. It is primarily residential and has a number of turn-of-the-century town houses in the Hamilton Heights Historic District. A branch of City College is nearby. **Washington Heights** The two rocky ridges that run through Manhattan and support its skyscrapers rise to a peak in Washington Heights. This was the strategic and important high ground George Washington occupied but failed to hold in 1776. Manhattan's highest point—267 feet—is in Bennett Park, bordered by 183rd and 185th Streets, Fort Washington, and Pinehurst Avenue. Bennett Park was once the estate of *New York Herald* publisher James Gordon Bennett. Once an Irish neighborhood, the area from Trinity Cemetery north to Dyckman Street now has a mixture of Irish, Latinos, African Americans, Greeks, and Armenians.

Audubon Terrace In 1841, after publishing his successful *Birds of America*, John James Audubon purchased the 24 acres along the Hudson River that now comprise Audubon Terrace, officially the Audubon Heights Museum Group. This is an odd mixture of a museum complex at West 155th Street and Broadway surrounded by tenements and housing projects. To the north and east is the Jumel Terrace Historic District. The museums here include the **American Numismatic Society (212/234-3130)**; the **Hispanic Society of America (212/928-2234)**, which contains an important collection of Spanish art; the **Puerto Rican Museum for the Arts (212/222-1966)**; and the **Academy of Arts and Letters (212/368-5900)**.

Fort Tryon Park This is the site of Fort Tryon, a Revolutionary fort that was the northernmost defense of Fort Washington. But most people come here to visit the Cloisters, which houses the medieval collection of the Metropolitan Museum of Art. Just to the south of the Cloisters in the St. Frances Cabrini Chapel, where the body of Mother Cabrini, the patron saint of immigrants, lies.

Inwood Hill Park At the northern end of Manhattan Island, Inwood Hill Park has playing fields and open parkland with views of the Hudson and the George Washington Bridge.

Harlem The first settlers were Dutch farmers who in 1672 put their slaves to work building a road (which later became Broadway) from Nieuw Haarlem, as the area was called, to Nieuw Amsterdam, ten miles to the south. The road encouraged wealthy farmers to build country estates, but Harlem didn't really open up until the coming of the railroad in 1837. In 1879 and 1880 the Third and Second Avenue elevated railways extended their lines to Harlem. This had the effect of splitting Harlem in two: East Harlem became a place of tenements for new European immigrants while West Harlem became a residential area for the rich. Oscar Hammerstein, Henry Morgenthau, and William B. Astor had homes there.

The financial panic of 1904 was a turning point in West Harlem. Many well-to-do white property owners sold out just as blacks in search of better housing were gravitating to the area. Blacks were first allowed to buy property in the St. Nicholas district, in 1919. During the 1920s the black population of Harlem more than doubled to over 200,000. Harlem became *the* black community in the country. Waves of blacks poured in from the South, often in need of jobs while lacking in education and skills. Urban renewal in the 1950s cleared many blocks of slums and replaced them with housing projects. Gentrification began in the 1970s as middle-class families moved into Striver's Row in the St. Nicholas district and the Mount Morris Park historic district.

Harlem occupies six square miles, from West 110th Street north to the Harlem River and bounded on the east by the East River. Many Latinos, particularly Puerto Ricans, have settled in East Harlem (the area east of Fifth Avenue), and a later wave of Dominicans and Cubans have settled along upper Broadway.

The Outer Boroughs

New York City's outer boroughs—The Bronx, Staten Island, Brooklyn, and Queens—gave up their independent status in 1898 under the Greater New York Charter. Though often overlooked, they are rich in history and have their own unique areas to counteract the image of being a mere urban extension of Manhattan.

The Bronx The Bronx was first settled in 1639 by Jonas Bronck, a Swedish sea captain in the service of the Dutch. He purchased land, which today is only a small part of the borough on the Harlem River, and called it Bronckland and the waterway on its eastern boundary Bronck's River. The settlement disbanded with his death in 1643.

The next settlers were led by the religious dissenter Anne Hutchinson, who had been exiled from Boston, and John Throckmorton, an outcast Anabaptist. They and small groups of followers settled in the East Bronx in 1844. Indians killed the people in Hutchinson's colony and forced Throckmorton's group to seek safety in New Amsterdam. Their names are remembered in the Hutchinson River Parkway and Throg's Neck.

The Bronx grew slowly until the 1840s, when Irish and German railroad workers began to settle there. They were displaced by other immigrants—Jews, Poles, Italians, and Greeks. The borough of the Bronx was created by the Greater New York Charter in 1898, with boundaries of the Hudson River and Long Island Sound, the Harlem River and Westchester County. For the next 50 years, the Bronx developed into a series of tightly knit and stable ethnic neighborhoods. Since World War II, though, changes have been brought about by an increasing mobility of the population, a changing economy, an influx of poorer minorities, and declining city services, all combining to change the character of the Bronx. Recent progress has helped stabilize the borough, but the South Bronx remains one of the city's major slums. Among the attractions of the Bronx today are Yankee Stadium, the Hall of Fame of Great Americans, Fordham University, the New York Botanical Garden, and the deservedly famous Bronx Zoo.

Riverdale Along the Hudson, from Spuyten Duyvil to the Westchester County border, is an affluent enclave called Riverdale. Among its treasures are Wave Hill, the boy-hood home of Theodore Roosevelt at 675 West 252nd Street, (718/549-3200), the Edgar Allan Poe Cottage at Grand Concourse and Kingsbridge Road (718/881-8900), and the Valentine-Varian House, which was occupied by the British during the Revolution and is now the Museum of Bronx History, 3266 Bainbridge Road (718/881-8900).

City Island The most uncharacteristic part of the Bronx is City Island, on Long Island Sound. Settled in 1685 and only 1½ miles wide, it was a shipbuilding and commercial fishing center. Now City Island is packed with marinas and seafood restaurants and offers visitors a slice of New England-style maritime recreation.

Queens Across the East River from Manhattan is a patchwork quilt of ethnic neighborhoods. Originally a handful of towns, Queens, like the Lower East Side a century ago, is today a destination for thousands of immigrants. In fact, a third of Queens residents are foreign-born.

Queens County was named for Queen Catherine, the wife of Charles II. It joined New York as a borough in 1898, the same year as Brooklyn and Staten Island. It was still a fairly rural area then with a population of 150,000. After the Queensboro Bridge was built in 1909 and the subway was extended to Queens the following year, Queens became a residential satellite of Manhattan. A continuous building boom merged the separate towns into one sprawling urban area buffered only by parks and enormous cemeteries.

Beginning in 1919, Queens was briefly the movie capital of the country, producing films with stars like the Marx Brothers, Gloria Swanson, and Rudolph Valentino. Astoria Studios (Thirty-fifth Avenue between 34th and 38th Streets) was run by Famous Players Corp. until it was taken over by Paramount Pictures.

Queens is the city's largest (118 square miles) and flattest borough, which explains why both of the city's major airports, La Guardia and Kennedy, are here and why the World's Fairs of 1939–40 and 1964–65 were held here. Shea Stadium, the home of the Mets, and the National Tennis Center, where the U.S. Open championships are held, are in the Flushing Meadows–Corona Park section, where the World's Fairs were held.

🎌
....

Back to the Futurama: Revisiting Relics of the World's Fairs

The first World's Fair, the one with the Trylon and Perisphere, was more fun than the one in 1964. In 1939 Americans believed in the future. The Futurama ride at the GM pavilion was the hit of the fair. Other favorites: Billy Rose's Aquacade, the Life Savers Parachute Tower, the 10-million-volt flash at the GE pavilion, and Raymond Loewy's streamlined train.

The 1964 fair tried hard, but somehow the magic was gone. The Unisphere took the place of the Trylon and Perisphere. The Vatican pavilion displayed Michelango's *Pieta*. GM had another Futurama, the IBM pavilion was egg-shaped, and Belgian waffles were popular.

The Queens Museum, housed in the New York City building of both fairs, has a permanent exhibition on both fairs. A panorama of the city of New York, a scale model of the city from the '64 fair, has been modernized with 60,000 additions. In Flushing Meadows–Corona Park, off the Grand Central Parkway, you can see the Unisphere, which has been refurbished and looks as good as new, and the surrounding fountains still shoot 22-foot jets of water. The Hall of Science in the park has been given a $12 million update. Walking tours and lectures on the fair are available through the museum. The Hall of Science is open from noon to 5 P.M. daily except Monday. Admission is $4 for adults, $2 for students and seniors. Free admission Wednesday and Thursday, 3 to 5 p.m. **Bounded by Van Wyck Expressway and 111th Street and Union Turnpike and the Port Washington branch of the Long Island Railroad.** ☎ 718/592-9700

If you'd like a World's Fair collectible, Mood Indigo has interesting items from both fairs. 181 Prince Street (Sullivan–Thompson Streets) 212/254-1176. Darrow's Fun Antiques also has fair memorabilia. 1101 First Avenue (60th–61st Street) 212/838-0730

Brooklyn Brooklyn was settled in the mid-1600s on land purchased from the Indians by the Dutch, who named it Breukelen, their word for "broken land." In 1642 Cornelis Dircksen began a rowboat service across the East River to a landing just north of Brooklyn Heights that became known as "Old Ferry." This same land was used by Washington in 1776 to evacuate his men to Manhattan after losing the Battle of Long Island.

When Robert Fulton introduced his new steam ferry on the East River in 1814, entrepreneurs began to transform Brooklyn into one of the world's first commuter sub-urbs. Brooklyn Heights, on a hill above the river, was promoted as the ideal residence for well-to-do New Yorkers. In 1834, overcoming the opposition of New York City, the City of Brooklyn was chartered. At the time, Brooklyn had 21,000 residents, compared with more than 200,000 in New York City.

Despite its smaller size, Brooklyn had become a rich and powerful city; by 1800 it was the third largest in the country. Joining it to New York City required building the 1,595-foot Brooklyn Bridge, the greatest engineering feat of its time. A week after its opening on May 25, 1883, throngs of pedestrians, panicked by the delusion that

The Brooklyn Bridge

New York Harbor

the bridge was collapsing, rushed to get off the span, killing 12 people and injuring scores more in the stampede. The next year P. T. Barnum paraded 12 elephants over the bridge to prove its solidity.

In 1898 Brooklyn joined the other boroughs and voted to become part of Greater New York. The bridge had opened up sections of Brooklyn to development, particularly Park Slope, west of Prospect Park. The growth of Brooklyn was also stimulated by immigration, commerce, and the subway. Brooklyn continued to be a self-contained city with its own parks, museum, theaters, historic sites, and an independent state of mind. It has suffered some hard knocks since the end of World War II. The Brooklyn Navy Yard, which had employed 70,000 during the war,

closed in 1966, and the Brooklyn Dodgers departed for Los Angeles in 1957.

Brooklyn Heights The Esplanade is a promenade along Brooklyn's heights on land once occupied by the Canarsie Indians. Since it opened in 1951 it has given pedestrians open space, salt-air breezes, and spectacular views of Lower New York and New York Harbor. These were the waters Robert Fulton's ferry crossed in 1814, encouraging landowners to break up their properties into building lots, thereby making Brooklyn Heights the first suburb of New York.

By 1847, when Henry Ward Beecher began preaching against slavery at the Plymouth Church of the Pilgrims at 175 Hicks Street,

Brooklyn Heights had become an area of elegance and upper-middle-class respectability. It has also been home to a number of literary figures, including Walt Whitman and, more recently, Arthur Miller and Norman Mailer.

Prospect Park Frederick Law Olmsted and Calvert Vaux believed that Prospect Park was their finest work, surpassing even Central Park in Manhattan. After the Civil War halted construction on an earlier plan, they took over in 1866 and worked on it until 1873. The Grand Army Plaza at the intersection of Flatbush Avenue and Prospect Park West features an 80-foot triumphal arch honoring Union soldiers. The Plaza entrance leads directly to the 75-acre Long Meadow.

Olmsted felt that Prospect Park was essential to the growth of Brooklyn, and he and Vaux hoped to link Prospect Park and Central Park with wide boulevards, a dream that was not realized. By the end of the nineteenth century, the park was receiving 10 million visitors a year. The 526-acre park is in west central Brooklyn, bounded by Eastern Parkway and Parkside Avenue, Washington and Ocean Avenues. For information: ☎ 718/438-0100.

Park Slope This residential area was developed after Prospect Park was completed, and streetcar lines were extended to the area in the 1880s. Park Slope has more than 1,000 buildings, with fine examples of the many architectural styles that flourished between the Civil War and World War I— Italianate, French Second Empire, Victorian, Gothic, and Queen, among others. Park Slope is now a historic district, bounded by Fourth and Flatbush Avenues and Prospect Park West.

Coney Island Vestiges remain of the once-fabulous entertainment complex that flourished from the time Steeplechase Park opened in 1897 until World War II. The 2½-mile boardwalk, which opened in 1921 shortly after the subway arrived, still remains. The awesome Cyclone, one of the ultimate roller-coaster rides, still operates, although the Parachute Jump, which moved here from the 1939 World's Fair, is an abandoned tower. Coney Island is bounded by Coney Island Creek, the Belt Parkway, Ocean Parkway, and the Atlantic Ocean.

Fort Hamilton This area has been a military installation since the Dutch built a blockhouse here in 1660, although they surrendered it to the British four years later. In 1776 American soldiers fired on the HMS *Asia* in an effort to damage the invading British fleet. During the War of 1812 Fort Lewis, an earth and timber fort on the site, joined the fort on Staten Island to prevent the British from attacking New York City. The cornerstone of Fort Hamilton, the first granite fort in the harbor, was laid in 1825. Over the years it has housed, trained, and processed troops and officers, including

The Staten Island Ferry

Robert E. Lee, Thomas "Stonewall" Jackson, and Abner Doubleday. During World War I the Narrows were guarded against submarines by a steel cable stretched between Fort Hamilton and Staten Island. Fort Hamilton can be toured. For information: ☎ 718/630-4349.

Staten Island The most remote and least populous borough, Staten Island would like to secede from New York City. Islanders argue that New York City takes their taxes to pay for its problems and gives them nothing but garbage. (Fresh Kills landfill, on the western side of the island, is one of the world's largest man-made structures.) To visit Staten Island's open spaces and handsome communities is to understand why the residents

would like to be free of the city's pressing problems.

Staten Island was one of the first places in America to be settled. Giovanni da Verrazano discovered the Narrows—the body of water separating the island from Brooklyn—in 1524, and his name graces the bridge that links the two boroughs today. Henry Hudson named the island "Staaten Eylandt" in 1609, and in 1687 the Duke of York sponsored a sailing competition with Staten Island as the prize. The Manhattan representatives won the race, and since then it has been governed from New York.

You can reach the island from Manhattan on the Staten Island Ferry. The ride from Battery Park in Lower Manhattan is free.

New York Firsts

The first St. Patrick's Day parade was held in 1766 by Irish soldiers serving in the British army.

The first organized baseball club in the city was the Knickerbockers, formed in 1845.

The first newspaper was the *New-York Gazette*; its first issue appeared November 5, 1725.

The first mayor was Thomas Willett, appointed by the English governor Richard Nicolls in 1665.

The first railroad was the New York and Harlem Railroad, which began service on November 24, 1832, connecting Union Square with 23rd Street and Fourth Avenue.

The first restaurant opened in 1831, when the Swiss brothers John and Peter Delmonico opened a small establishment on William Street.

The first chartered bank was the Bank of New York, which announced its opening on February 23, 1784, three months after the last British troops left the city.

The first settlers were Walloons who arrived in 1624 with the sponsorship of the Dutch West India Company.

The first institution of higher learning was King's College, which opened at Trinity Church on Wall Street in 1754. Closed during the Revolution, it reopened in 1784 as Columbia College.

The first literary description of Manhattan was written in 1524 by Giovanni da Verrazano: "After a hundred leagues we found a very agreeable place between two small but prominent hills. . . . The people . . . dressed in bird's feathers of various colors, and they came toward us joyfully, uttering loud cries of wonderment."

The first nonprofit educational museum was the Tammany Museum, founded in 1790 to collect Americana, including Indian artifacts.

The first bridge was the King's Bridge in 1693. It spanned Spuyten Duyvil Creek between Manhattan and what now is the Bronx.

The first radio broadcast was made in 1910. To demonstration his new invention, the "vacuum tube," Lee De Forest broadcast Enrico Caruso singing at the Metropolitan Opera House.

The first guidebook to the city was published in 1818 by A. T. Goodrich.

The first organized football game in the city was in 1870. Rutgers defeated Columbia University, six goals to three.

The first building in the country to be erected specifically for use as a hotel was probably the City Hotel, begun in 1794, on lower Broadway between Thames and Cedar Streets.

The first racetrack was the Newmarket Track at Salisbury Plain (now Hempstead), Long Island. It was built in 1655, by order of Governor Richard Nicolls.

The first recognized boxing match in the country was between Jacob Hyer and Tom Beasley in the city in 1816.

The first bar was the City Tavern (Stad Herbergh in Dutch), which sold wine and beer imported by the Dutch East India Company.

The first bookshop opened in 1693. It was run by William Bradford, the official printer of the colony.

The first tennis game in the country was played on a lawn court at the Staten Island Cricket and Baseball Club.

The first theater is believed to be the New Theatre (better known as the Nassau Street Theatre), which was built by English colonists around 1732.

The first international aviation races were sponsored by James Gordon Bennett Jr. in 1906.

The first opera was performed in the city in 1750, when the Nassau Street Theatre presented ballad operas, such as John Gay's *The Beggar's Opera*.

The first public library was the New York Society Library, founded in 1754.

The first municipal golf course in the country opened at Van Courtlandt Park in 1891.

The first fire department, a volunteer force of thirty "strong, able, discreet, honest, and sober men," was founded in 1737.

The first movie filmed in New York was the work of Charles E. Chinnock, a former employee of Thomas Edison, who invented the motion picture. Filmed on a Brooklyn rooftop, it showed a boxing match.

SPECIAL CITY SPOTS

Finding Tranquility in Historic Churches

The city's hustle and bustle can frazzle even the hardiest New Yorker. For quick relief, try slipping into an old church for a few minutes. It will help you regain your composure and sense of proportion. Here are some that have seen a lot of history:

St. Paul's Chapel
123 Broadway
(Fulton–Vesey Streets)

This is the oldest church still standing in Manhattan. It was built in 1766, in a wheat field overlooking the Hudson River. At first it seemed too far out of town for some parishioners. George Washington used to worship here in 1789, when the city was the capital of the United States.

St. Mark's Church-in-the-Bowery
Second Avenue at East 10th Street

Built in 1799 on the site of the farm of Peter Stuyvesant, the Dutch governor, this simple structure contains Stuyvesant's remains. In 1828, after the Bowery became more fashionable, the Greek Revival steeple was added.

St. Patrick's Old Cathedral
264 Mulberry Street
(Prince–East Houston)

Built in 1815 and rebuilt after a fire in 1868, this was the first St. Patrick's Cathedral in the city. St. Patrick's became a parish church in the Irish neighborhood after the cathedral moved to Fifth Avenue and 40th Street in 1879. The funeral for John F. Kennedy Jr. was held here.

Church of St. Luke-in-the-Fields
487 Hudson Street
(Barrow–Christopher Streets)

Parishioners sailed up the Hudson to worship in this church, built in 1822 in a field overlooking the river. The first church warden here was Clement C. Moore, who is remembered for writing the beloved poem *A Visit from St. Nicholas*. St. Luke's still has the feeling of a country church.

St. Peter's Church
22 Barclay Street (Church Street)

Built in 1785, this austere Greek Revival church was New York's first Roman Catholic church. Catholicism had been banned under British rule. An early parishioner was Pierre Toussaint, a former slave from Haiti who became a philanthropist and is now up for canonization.

Marble Collegiate Church
272 Fifth Avenue (West 29th Street)

This Gothic church stands unchanged since it was built in 1854. The clock is still wound by hand every eight days, and the racks behind the pews wait to hold your walking stick. The church was Dutch Reform—the oldest denomination in the city—and was established by Peter Minuit in 1628. The world-renowned Dr. Norman Vincent Peale was the pastor for decades.

Little Church Around the Corner
1 East 29th Street
(Madison–Fifth Avenues)

Officially this is the Church of the Transfiguration. When George Holland, an actor who lived in the neighborhood, died in 1870, a friend went to a nearby church to arrange for the funeral. "We don't accept actors here," he was told, "but there is a church around the corner that will." So an Episcopal church, built in 1849 in the quaint cottage Gothic style and set in a garden, was given a new name and a new reputation among actors, some of whom are memorialized here—Edwin Booth, Gertrude Lawrence, and Richard Mansfield, among others. During World War I and the years just after the war, this was the scene of more weddings than any other church in the world.

St. Patrick's Cathedral
Fifth Avenue at 50th Street

Everyone in the city knows St. Pat's: on Fifth Avenue, next to Saks and across from Rockefeller Center. Construction began in 1858, but it was halted by the Civil War and wasn't finished until 1879. At that time the church was considered too far uptown; now it is dwarfed by its surroundings. This is the eleventh-largest church in the world; the spires soar 330 feet, the window above the central portal is 26 feet in diameter, and the cathedral seats 2,400. More than half of its stained-glass windows were made in the French cities of Chartres and Nantes.

Cathedral of St. John the Divine
Amsterdam Avenue at West 112th Street

This neo-Byzantine edifice was begun in 1892 and isn't finished yet. After the cathedral was partially built, the design was modified in 1911 to reflect the new French Gothic fashion. Work was discontinued in 1941 and not resumed until the 1980s. When it is finished, it will be the largest cathedral in the world. The nave is 601 feet long and 146 feet wide; when completed the transepts will be just as wide and will span 320 feet. The

St. Patrick's Cathedral, the eleventh-largest church in the world

interior is spectacular, with seven chapels in a variety of styles. St. John is a bit big for quiet contemplation, but it certainly is worth seeing.

St. Bartholomew's Church
Park Avenue and East 50th Street

This Byzantine-style church with its charming little garden was built in 1919 where the Schaefer Brewery once stood. The Romanesque portal, designed by Stanford White in 1902, was brought here from the old St. Bartholomew's Church at Madison Avenue and 24th Street.

Temple Emanu-El
65th Street at Fifth Avenue

This is one of the largest synagogues in the world. The temple seats 2,500, 100 more than St. Patrick's. This gray limestone edifice is the temple of the oldest Reform congregation in New York. The hall is 77 feet wide, 150 feet long, and 403 feet high. When the temple was built in 1929, New York had the largest Jewish population of any city in the world.

Buildings That Speak of Past Glories

"The present in New York is so powerful that the past is lost," wrote the essayist and poet John Jay Chapman. True, a dynamic city is forever tearing down old buildings and building new ones, and true, no city is as dynamic as New York. But the city is rich in great old buildings, which each in its own way says something about the city's past. New York's past isn't lost, but we must know where to look for it.

Chrysler Building
405 Lexington Avenue
(East 42nd Street)

This classic art deco building still radiates American confidence and optimism. It was the world's tallest building for about nine months, between its completion in 1930 and the topping-off of the taller Empire State Building in 1931. Many still consider this the quintessential skyscraper, the unsurpassed symbol of New York sass. It was built for the Chrysler Corporation, and has many car-oriented elements—abstract friezes depicting automobiles, a spire modeled after a radiator grille. The lobby, another art deco treasure, was once used as a car showroom. The lighting of the spire at night was the idea of the architect, William Van Alen. After being discontinued for a time, the lighting was reinstituted in 1981. Many New Yorkers develop a personal relationship with the Chrysler Building, and if the lights don't go on precisely on time they phone to see what's wrong.

Grand Central Station
East 42nd Street and Park Avenue

In 1913, an architectural competition to build this terminus was won by the designs of Reed & Stern. The firm of Warren & Wetmore was hired to work on the Beaux Arts terminal. The main facade facing down Park Avenue includes triumphal arches filled with steel and glass, surmounted by a colossal clock and sculpture group that combines Roman deities and an American eagle. At the center of the facade is a bronze figure of Cornelius Vanderbilt, founder of the New York Central Railroad. Inside, the hall of the Main Concourse is 160 feet wide, 470 feet long, and 140 feet high at its apogee. The ceiling is decorated with a zodiac representing the winter sky. The terminal has been

recently cleaned and restored and is beautiful. (Tours of Grand Central are conducted by the Municipal Arts Society for a small fee. They meet in the Main Concourse on Wednesdays at 12:30 P.M. For tour information phone 212/935-3960.

The Plaza
58th–59th Streets and Grand Army Plaza

This 1907 Edwardian-French *grand dame* was designed by Henry J. Hardenbergh, who also designed the Dakota apartments. The site is unique: two sides of the building are equally exposed. From the beginning The Plaza was the center of social activity in the city. It has hosted presidents, visiting royalty, the Beatles, F. Scott Fitzgerald and his wife, Zelda, who, the story goes, once danced nude in the fountain out front. For years Solomon R. Guggenheim resided in the State Suite surrounded by paintings from his collection. Part of what makes The Plaza so magnificent is its setting on the **Grand Army Plaza,** which acts both as a forecourt to the hotel to the south and an entrance terrace to Central Park to the north. The fountain,

(Opposite) The Empire State Building, one of New York's most famous landmarks
(Below) Grand Central Station

designed by Carrere & Hastings, was built with a bequest from newspaper magnate Joseph Pulitzer. The equestrian statue of William Tecumseh Sherman by Augustus Saint-Gaudens was displayed at the World Exhibition in Paris in 1900.

The Dakota
1 West 72nd Street
(Central Park West)

When this luxury apartment house was built in 1884, its owner, Edgar Clark, president of the Singer Sewing Company, remarked that it was so far out of town, "it might as well be in Dakota Territory." The idea appealed to him and he instructed the architect, Henry J. Hardenbergh, to embellish the buildings with symbols of the West—arrowheads, sheaves of wheat, and ears of corn. The highly original building has elements of German Renaissance and Romanesque architecture, and has turrets, gables, oriels, dormers, and pinnacles. The Dakota was the setting for the film *Rosemary's Baby*. It has been the home of Judy Garland, Lauren Bacall, Leonard Bernstein, Roberta Flack, and John Lennon, who, in 1980, was shot to death at the building's entrance.

Woolworth Building
233 Broadway
(Park Place–Barclay Street)

When completed in 1913, this building, the headquarters of Frank W. Woolworth's chain of five-and-dime stores, was described as a "cathedral of commerce." Its neo-

Gothic style does suggest a church building. Its picturesque details enhance the graceful, vertical thrust, which culminates in a crown. There are interesting details inside, including a caricatural bas-relief that shows the architect, Cass Gilbert, with a model of the building, and another of Woolworth counting nickels and dimes. Woolworth was so pleased with the building that he paid for it in cash—$1.5 million.

City Hall
City Hall Park
(Park Row–Broadway)

This Federal-style building with French Renaissance details has been the city's seat of government since it opened on July 4, 1811, a surprising example of continuity in a city known for constant change. Designed by Joseph Mangin and John McComb Jr., who won $350 for submitting the winning plans in an architectural competition, it also is one of the city's most architecturally distinguished buildings. Inside, the rotunda has a sweeping twin-spiral staircase. Horace Greeley, Ulysses S. Grant, and Abraham Lincoln all lay in state in the rotunda, and some 60,000 people followed Lincoln's coffin up Broadway. On the second floor, the Governor's Room is now an art gallery and can be visited by the public. Among the American paintings on display is a portrait of George Washington on Evacuation Day, Nov. 24, 1783. City Hall was built facing south, because the city fathers at the time doubted that the

New York Public Library

city would extend much farther
north. The small park was the
city's village green in colonial days,
and it still visually enhances City
Hall. The park includes an 1890
statue of Nathan Hale, who before
being hanged by the British, pro-
claimed: "I regret that I have but
one life to lose for my country." A
plaque at 44th and Vanderbilt
Avenue marks the spot where Hale
was hanged.

Ansonia Hotel
2109 Broadway
(West 73rd–74th Streets)

This Beaux-Arts wedding cake was
designed by the millionaire who
built it, William Earl Dodge Stokes,
heir to the Phelps Dodge Copper
and Ansonia Brass and Copper
fortunes. The detailing on the
building is unusually rich—corner

turrets, ornate balconies, and terra-
cotta trim. It was built with excep-
tionally thick walls, which made it
virtually soundproof. As a result,
the Ansonia has been popular with
musicians and singers—Enrico
Caruso, Yehudi Menuhin, Ezio
Pinza, Igor Stravinsky, and Arturo
Toscanini have all lived here at various times since the building was
completed in 1904. Originally, live
seals played in a fountain in the
lobby.

New York Public Library
Fifth Avenue at 42nd Street

When this Beaux Arts landmark
was built in 1911 on the site of
the old Croton Reservoir, it cost $9
million, a huge sum in those days,
but it was worth every penny.
The Carrere & Hastings design
included the long forecourt along

Fifth Avenue, where E. C. Potter's sculptural lions now stand guard. The interior, with its grand staircase, vaulted ceilings, murals, white marble walls, and paneled reading rooms, is one of the great public spaces in the city. Today the building houses a research collection, formed in 1895 from the Lenox and Astor libraries plus funds from the trust of former governor Samuel J. Tilden. The literary treasures here rank with those of the Library of Congress. On the west side of the library, stretching to Sixth Avenue, is the 9.6-acre Bryant Park, once a potter's field. It later was the site of a Crystal Palace, erected for the World's Fair of 1853.

Seagram Building
375 Park Avenue
(East 52nd–53rd Streets)

It is incomprehensible that Mies van der Rohe's magnificent bronze and bronze-glass structure is more than 40 years old; it looks as fresh and exciting as it did when it was completed in 1958. This is the building that reintroduced the idea of a plaza to the city, and the building everyone copied. It is still the best, classically proportioned and exquisitely detailed. Phyllis Lambert, daughter of the chairman of the board, Edgar Bronfman, was the catalyst. She brought all the architectural standards learned at Vassar to her father. Love and respect for his daughter allowed the construction of a modern masterpiece.

Rockefeller Center
West 48th to West 51st Streets
(Fifth–Sixth Avenues)

This is the world's largest privately owned business and entertainment complex, with 19 buildings covering 21 acres. It began in 1928 when John D. Rockefeller Jr. bought up leases on land in the area to provide a new setting for the Metropolitan Opera House. The opera backed out when the Depression came, leaving the philanthropist with a long-term lease on 11.7 midtown acres. He decided to go it alone, and demolition of 228 buildings began in May 1931 to make way for the project. The original 14 buildings were completed by April 1940, with the crown jewel being the 70-story RCA Building, now the GE Building. A favorite over the years has been Radio City Music Hall, built for variety shows but soon converted to a 5,882-seat movie theater, which also had stage shows featuring the Rockettes, the Corps de Ballet, the Symphony Orchestra, and a variety of guest artists. Rockefeller Center is still a vital and handsome part of the city, but the best part of it all is the thought of Rockefeller—at the depth of the Depression, with part of Central Park a shanty town and once-prosperous businessmen selling apples on street corners—deciding to go it alone, to develop his dream by himself. It is that audacity that makes New York the most exciting city in the world.

Rockefeller Center at Christmas

Nine Classic City Hotels

Great cities have great hotels, and New York has its full share. Most of the ones described here are *grand dames*, upholding standards that date from the turn of the twentieth century. A handful of new hotels are also great—the Peninsula, Plaza-Athenee, Box Tree, Morgans, Royalton—but they are hardly retro.

The Algonquin
59 West 44th Street
(Fifth–Sixth Avenues)
☎ 212/840-6800

Built in 1902, this hotel, at the eastern edge of the theater district, became a rendezvous for theater and literary figures. In the 1920s, its Rose Room housed America's most famous luncheon, the Round Table, habituated by F. P. Adams, Robert Benchley, Harold Ross, Alexander Wolcott, Dorothy Parker, and others. Few places are as comfortable as the Algonquin lobby, where you can summon a waiter by ringing a bell. Many actors and actresses stay here while appearing on Broadway. With only 165 rooms, it resembles a country inn more than it does a large-city hotel.

Carlyle Hotel
35 East 76th Street
(Madison Avenue)
☎ 212/744-1600

Built just before the Crash of 1929, this comfortable, elegant hotel became the New York headquarters for both the Truman and the Kennedy administrations. Both presidents usually stayed here while visiting the city. The artist Ludwig Bemelmans decorated the bar, and Bobby Short has made the Cafe Carlyle synonymous with urban sophistication. Small by New York standards, the Carlyle's 38 stories contain only 180 guest rooms.

Lowell Hotel
28 East 63rd Street (Park–Madison)
☎ 212/838-1400

This small 1926 gem manages to be both luxurious and charming. Many of its 65 rooms and suites have wood-burning fireplaces and serving pantries. The suites have garden terraces. Understandably

The Ten Tallest Buildings

New York is inextricably associated with skyscrapers and has more of them than any other city in the world. Manhattan Island is a giant rock, which permits buildings to soar, their height limited only by man's imagination and technology.

The demand for tall office buildings arose during the 1860s as the commercial district along Broadway between the Battery and City Hall became more congested, and large businesses sought more impressive headquarters.

A view of the Empire State Building at night

What made the early skyscrapers possible was the invention of the passenger elevator. The Equitable Building, 7½ stories tall, opened the age of the skyscraper. By 1875 the city had several ten-story buildings, notably the Western Union building and the Tribune building.

Each of these buildings was once the tallest in the world.

The building of tall buildings has continued unabated through the years, and in 1990 New York had 24 of the 100 tallest buildings in the world.

These buildings were all the tallest in the world when they were built:

World Trade Towers (1973)	1,350 ft.
Empire State Building (1931)	1,250
Chrysler Building (1929)	1,048
Woolworth Building (1913)	792
MetLife Tower (1909)	699
Singer Building (1908)	612 *
Park Row Building (1899)	386
St. Patrick's Cathedral (1888)	330
Trinity Church (1846)	281
St. Paul's Chapel (1794)	220

* This building has been torn down.

The Plaza Hotel

popular with British actors and actresses appearing on Broadway. The Pembroke Room serves breakfast and afternoon tea. The Post House restaurant on the second floor is excellent.

The Plaza
Fifth Avenue at Grand Army Plaza
(West 58th–West 59th Streets)
☎ 212/759-3000

This vestige of Edwardian elegance is the masterpiece of architect Henry J. Hardenbergh, who also designed the Dakota. The Plaza has hosted Teddy Roosevelt, F. Scott and Zelda Fitzgerald, and practically everyone who was anyone visiting New York. Frank Lloyd Wright was a devotee of The Plaza and used it as his New York headquarters. Rooms on the north side have dramatic views of Central Park. Eloise, the popular creation of author Kay Thompson, lived here. New Yorkers come to have a drink in the Oak Bar, take high tea in Palm Court, and dine in the Edwardian Room.

The Pierre
2 East 61st Street (Fifth Avenue)
☎ 212/838-8000

This grand European-style hotel debuted in 1930 and was an immediate hit with the rich and the powerful. It is arguably the most sophisticated hotel in the city. The 202 rooms are enormous, and the ones on the upper floors have views of Central Park. The staff is attentive and will unpack for you. Afternoon tea is served in the handsome Rotunda, and the Cafe Pierre is a delightful place to dine.

St. Regis
2 East 55th Street (Fifth Avenue)
☎ 212/753-4500

John Jacob Astor told his architects he wanted the finest hotel in the world, a place where guests would feel as comfortable as they did in a gracious private home. Completed in 1904, the St. Regis has been living up to Mr. Astor's standards ever since. A $100 million renovation, completed in 1991, has made this a state-of-the-art hotel, now part of the ITT Sheraton's Luxury Collection. Where once there were 500 rooms, there are now 322, 86 of them suites. The King Cole Bar, dominated by the Maxfield Parrish mural of King Cole's court, is an elegant meeting place.

Sherry-Netherland Hotel
781 Fifth Avenue (59th Street)
☎ 212/355-2800

Louis Sherry, of ice cream fame, built this elegant hotel in 1927, and its high-peaked roof and gargoyles suggest a chateau in the Loire Valley. Panels rescued from a Vanderbilt mansion grace the walls lining the entrance. The 54-room hotel was closed for two years in the early 1990s while it underwent a two-year, $18 million renovation. The rooms are particularly large, the service impeccable.

Dining at the Waldorf-Astoria

The Stanhope
995 Fifth Avenue (East 81st Street)
☎ 212/288-5800

This hotel, built in 1926, is just across Fifth Avenue from the Metropolitan Museum of Art, and is a gracious haven for those who seek refuge from midtown. Its 148 rooms, most of which are suites, are elegantly decorated with Louis XV-style antiques with Asian accents in the French style. High tea is, of course, British. In the summer, the Terrace is a perfect place to sip an aperitif and people-watch. The hotel has limousine service to Lincoln Center and the theater district.

Waldorf-Astoria
30 Park Avenue
(East 49th–50th Streets)
☎ 212/355-3000

This hotel was world-famous before it moved here from its original site, which is where the Empire State Building now rises. Rich guests (and President Franklin D. Roosevelt) used to arrive underground in their private railway cars on a spur of the tracks under Park Avenue. Built in the art deco style, the public spaces were redone in the Edwardian style in the early 1960s. The 625-foot Waldorf Towers, with 118 guest rooms and 77 suites, have been home to Herbert Hoover, General Douglas MacArthur, the Duke and Duchess of Windsor, Henry Kissinger, and Cole Porter. High tea in Peacock Alley is a delight.

A Dozen Fascinating Small Museums

Everyone knows the Met, MOMA, and the Guggenheim. They're too big to ignore. But the city is rich in museums— around a hundred, if you count all five boroughs and take a liberal view of what constitutes a museum. For many, their very smallness is a virtue; in an hour or so, you can see something old and learn something new. These museums will take you back in time, and you'll return to the present refreshed.

Ellis Island Museum of Immigration

Take the Statue of Liberty Ferry from Castle Clinton in Battery Park; the ferry fee ($7 for adults, $3 for children 3 to 17) includes a round trip to Ellis Island and the Statue of Liberty.

☎ 212/363-3267

The first immigrant, an Irish girl named Annie Moore, came through Ellis Island in 1892, and more than 16 million followed her before it was closed in 1932. Visitors can now follow the footsteps of their ancestors, from the Baggage Room, where they dropped off what was often all their worldly belongings, to the Registry Room, where they underwent a short medical exam and a 30-question legal exam, to the staircase that led to the ferryboat that took them to New York. See *Island of Tears*, a film that documents the immigrant experience; Treasures from Home, a collection of personal property of the immigrants; and the American Immigrant Hall of Honor, inscribed with the names of more than 420,000 commemorated by their descendants through a donation to the Statue of Liberty–Ellis Island Foundation (212/883-1986). In the Oral History Studio listen to immigrants reminisce about their experience here. The museum is open daily, 9:30 A.M. to 3 P.M.

South Street Seaport Museum

12 Fulton Street (South Street)

☎ 212/748-6500

Actually, this museum is an 11-square-block historic district, but most people don't realize it because it's so much fun. It was founded in 1867 to preserve, interpret, and display the city's history as a world port. The museum has restored buildings, a working nineteenth-century print shop, boat-building shop, a maritime-crafts center, children's center,

A scene from Ellis Island

library, historic art and archaeological collections, and two museum shops. The museum's "fleet" includes two National Historic Landmarks: the *Lettie G. Howard*, an 1893 fishing schooner, and the *Ambrose*, a 1908 lightship. The seaport has a number of restaurants along the pier. Special events include concerts, children's programs, and harbor tours. The museum is open daily from 10 A.M. to 5 P.M. and to 6 P.M. in the summer. Admission is $6 for adults, $5 for seniors, $4 for students, and $3 for children under 12.

Forbes Magazine Galleries
62 Fifth Avenue (12th Street)
☎ 212/206-5548

Millionaire publisher Malcolm Forbes was an enthusiastic and incurable collector, and these galleries hold exhibits drawn from his collections. "The World of Faberge," for example, contains more than 300 objets d'art, including eight imperial Easter eggs created by Peter Carl Faberge. "Important American Historical Papers" include George Washington's handwritten reminiscences of his military career and Paul Revere's expense account for his famous ride. A personal favorite is

"Toy Boats & Toy Soldiers." The museum is open Tuesday, Wednesday, Friday, and Saturday. Hours vary; call first. Free admission.

Morgan Library
29 East 36th Street
(Madison Avenue)
☎ 212/685-0610

At the turn of the twentieth century, this was the home of J. Pierpont Morgan, the greatest financier in America. He had been a collector from the time he went abroad to school in 1854. He was wealthy and bought what he liked, although it was not until 1890, when his banker father was killed, that he began to collect in earnest, and on a grand scale. He bought a Gutenberg Bible, Shakespeare folios, and manuscripts by Keats, Dickens, and Byron. In ten years his collection had become so large that to house it he commissioned the noted architect Charles F. McKim to build this Renaissance palazzo, now one of the city's classic monuments. When he died in 1913, the Morgan Library, the finest private library in the country, was his legacy. Of particular interest to non-scholars is Morgan's study, known as the West Room. Here he was host to royalty, politicians, ecclesiastical figures, foreign dignitaries, collectors, scholars, and the group of bankers that Morgan assembled to stem the financial panic of 1907. The library is open from 10:30 A.M. to 5 P.M. Tuesdays to Thursdays, 10:30 A.M. to 8 P.M. Fridays, 10:30 A.M. to 6 P.M.

Saturdays, and noon to 6 P.M. Sundays. Admission $7 for adults, $5 for seniors and students. Both the Court Cafe and the Library Shop are excellent.

Museum of Television and Radio
25 West 52nd Street
(Fifth–Sixth Avenues)
☎ 212/621-6800

Founded in 1975 by William Paley of CBS, this museum collects and preserves tapes of television and radio programs; its collection includes thousands of TV and radio programs, all available for viewing or listening. In the archives are news and public-affairs programs, documentaries, performing arts, children's programming, sports, comedy, drama, and advertising. There are daily screenings of programs like *Alfred Hitchcock Presents*, presidential commercials, and early talk shows. A radio listening room gives the listener access to a vanished era. The museum is open from noon to 6 P.M. Tuesday and Wednesday, noon to 8 P.M. Thursday, and noon to 6 P.M. Friday through Sunday. Admission is $4 for adults, $3 students, $2 seniors and children under 13.

Society of Illustrators Museum of American Illustration
128 East 63rd Street
(Lexington Avenue)
☎ 212/838-2560

If you enjoy the great illustrators like Norman Rockwell, N. C. Wyeth, Maxfield Parrish, Charles Dana Gibson, and James Mont-

USS *Intrepid*

gomery Flagg, you will find them well represented here. Displayed throughout the 1875 East Side town house are items from the society's collection of more than 2,000 works created from 1838 to the present. Two galleries display exhibits on both historical and contemporary themes. Occasional lectures and auctions are open to the public. The museum, which includes a gift shop, is open from 10 A.M. to 8 P.M. Tuesday, 10 A.M. to 5 P.M. Wednesday through Friday, and noon to 4 P.M. Saturday; closed in August and on major holidays. Admission is free.

Intrepid Sea-Air-Space Museum
Pier 86 (West 46th Street–Twelfth Avenue)
☎ 212/245-0072

This aircraft carrier, a veteran of World War II and Vietnam, is now a historical and technological museum, a worthy counterpart to the Air and Space Museum in Washington, D.C., and the next best thing to going to sea with the Navy. You can inspect fighters and other aircraft on the 900-foot flight deck, climb through control bridges and command centers, see film clips of early flying machines in Pioneers Hall, and look into the future of flight and ocean exploration in Technologies Hall. Tied up next to the carrier are the guided-missile submarine *Growler* and the Vietnam-era destroyer *Edison*. All ships are open from 10 A.M. to 5 P.M. Tuesday to Sunday; closed Tuesdays in winter. Admission: adults $10, seniors and veterans $7.50, children under 12 $5, free for children under 6 and for uniformed servicemen. The museum includes a gift shop, snack bar, and picnic facilities.

Museum of American Folk Art
2 Lincoln Square
(West 65th Street–Columbus Avenue)
☎ 212/977-7298

If you love quilts and tinware and weathervanes and Shaker boxes and decoys and whirligigs and hand-carved toys and wooden Indians and samplers and Grandma Moses paintings and all the other things that are called folk art, they are here in abundance. The museum was founded in 1961 to preserve the rich American folk art tradition though exhibitions, educational programs, and publications, including the museum's outstanding magazine, *Folk Art*. Changing exhibits draw on the museum's extensive permanent collection. This is a great place to visit before or after a matinee at Lincoln Center, which is across the street. The museum is open from 11:30 A.M. to 7:30 P.M. Tuesday to Sunday, except on major holidays. In addition, the museum sponsors occasional performances by folk musicians and operates an excep-

tional gift shop next door. Admission is free.

American Museum–Hayden Planetarium
West 79th Street and Central Park West
☎ 212/769-5100

More than 30 million people have visited this planetarium since it opened in the late 1930s. The big attraction is the Sky Theater, which presents daily Sky Shows and a laser-light show on Friday and Saturday evenings. There are many permanent exhibits, including the Hall of the Sun, antique astronomical instruments, and art displays in the Black Arts Gallery. The Guggenheim Space Theater has slide shows that simultaneously use 22 screens. The planetarium is open from October through June. The American Museum of Natural History, through which you enter the planetarium, is open from 10 A.M. to 5:45 P.M. Sunday to Thursday, 10 A.M. to 8:45 P.M. Friday and Saturday. A restaurant and cafeteria are in the museum, along with a gift shop. Admission: adults $8, students and seniors $6, children 12 and under $4.50. (Note: The Hayden Planetarium at the Rose Center for Earth and Space opened in February of 2000. Call 212/769-5100 for schedule.)

New-York Historical Society
2 West 77th Street
(Central Park West)
☎ 212/873-3400

This venerable institution was founded in 1804, when New York was still hyphenated. The organization's first home was City Hall; seven moves later it found a handsome permanent home on the Upper West Side. Everyone who is interested in the city will find something of interest—historical prints, portraits, rare maps, sculpture and the decorative arts, all of which are of outstanding quality. Exceptional items include George Washington's inaugural carriage, Audubon's original watercolors for his *Birds of America*, the country's largest collection of Tiffany lamps, the original model of the ironclad *Monitor*, and the correspondence between Aaron Burr and Alexander Hamilton that led to their duel. The eight miles of shelf space in the society's research library are filled with more than 650,000 books, two million manuscripts, 35,000 maps and atlases, 15,000 pieces of sheet music, and 40,000 broadsides. And if there were nothing else here, you should come to see Thomas Cole's *The Course of Empire*, his 1836 series of five paintings, which is on display with other works by artists of the Hudson River School. The site also includes a gift shop. Hours: 11 A.M. to 5 P.M. Tuesday to Sunday; closed major holidays. Admission: adults $5, seniors and students $3, children 12 and under $1.

International Center of Photography

1130 Fifth Avenue
(East 94th Street)
☎ 212/860-1777

Photography is now recognized as an art, and this center, founded by photographer Cornell Capa, has become the most influential institution in both photographic art and photojournalism. It is housed in a four-story, red brick Federal town house, and contains the Photography Hall of Fame, which honors those who have made significant contributions to the art and science of professional photography. Since the opening of the center in late 1974, it has shown the works of more than 300 photographers, including one-person shows by Henri Cartier-Bresson, Weegee, Robert Capa (Cornell's brother), and W. Eugene Smith. The center also has a gallery at 1133 Sixth Avenue (West 43rd Street), 212/722-5234. The center is open from 10 A.M. to 5 P.M. Tuesday to Thursday, 10 A.M. to 8 P.M. Friday, 10 A.M. to 6 P.M. Saturday and Sunday. The center includes a gift shop. Admission: adults $6, seniors and students $4.

American Museum of the Moving Image

35-01 35th Avenue (36th Street), Queens
☎ 718/784-0077

This museum was created for movie buffs. Located in Queens, in a building that in the 1920s was the East Coast production facility for Paramount Pictures, it offers rotating exhibitions, old movie sets, and daily screenings. Its collection includes more than 70,000 artifacts that trace the art and technology of motion pictures and television. The ground floor houses a gallery and an imaginative gift shop. The second floor houses Behind the Screen, which is the museum's permanent collection. The rest of the Astoria Studio Complex gives a behind-the-scenes look at various aspects of filmmaking—editing, sound, costumes, marketing and promotion, set design and construction, produc-

ing, makeup, lighting, and more. The museum is open from noon to 4 P.M. Tuesday to Friday, 11 to 6 on weekends. The grounds include a gift shop, a cafe area with vending machines, and picnic facilities. Admission: adults $8.50, seniors $5.50, students with ID and children 5 to 18 $4.50.

Visiting Historic Houses Around the City

In a city like New York, private houses are at the mercy of progress and are constantly being torn down to make room for new buildings. Not surprisingly, only a few historic houses remain. One way to escape the pressures of the present is to visit some of these treasures and to learn about the people who once lived in them.

MANHATTAN

The Old Merchant's House
19 East 4th Street (at the Bowery)
☎ 212/777-1089
The street where this house stands was once one of the most fashionable in the city, and is lined with beautiful town houses. This house

is one of the city's finest examples of Greek Revival architecture. It was left exactly as it was when, in 1835, a merchant named Seabury Tredwell moved into the house. When Gertrude Tredwell, Seabury's last descendant, died in 1933, the house was scheduled for public auction. George Chapman, a distant relative, created the Historic

Landmark Society to save the house. Open from 1 to 4 P.M. Sunday to Thursday; closed on holidays and in August. Phone in advance. Admission: $5 for adults, $3 for students and seniors, children under 12 free.

Theodore Roosevelt Birthplace
28 East 20th Street
(Broadway–Park Avenue)
☎ 212/260-1616

Cornelius Roosevelt, the grandfather of the future president, purchased two adjoining houses on East 20th Street as wedding gifts for his two sons, and they lived there until 1892, when Teddy was 14. They moved uptown, and some years later the houses were demolished. In 1923 Teddy Roosevelt's birthplace was reconstructed as a memorial to the 26th president of the United States. The Gothic Revival house is a copy of the original in every detail, including the furnishings. Five rooms and two museums are open to the public. The array of memorabilia is staggering—diaries, bits of baby clothing, faded tintypes, zoological notebooks of his safaris, newspaper clippings, political cartoons, uniforms, bugles, mementos of the Inaugural Ball, relics of World War I, campaign buttons—the collection seems endless. The site, which includes a gift shop, is open from 9 A.M. to 5 P.M. daily, closed Mondays, Tuesdays, and all federal holidays. Admission $2.

Abigail Adams Smith Museum
421 East 61st Street
(York–First Avenues)
☎ 212/838-6878

This landmark was originally a carriage house on the estate of Colonel William Stephens Smith, aide-de-camp to George Washington and the husband of Abigail Adams, daughter of President John Adams. The house is set on a high embankment about 10 feet above the 61st Street exit off East River Drive. Once known as "Smith's Folly," the estate dates from 1795, and was considered one of the finest estates in Manhattan. In the early 1900s, the property was purchased by the Colonial Dames of America, who now make their headquarters here and maintain the exhibition rooms—the music room, dining room, bedrooms, and parlors. Most of the authentic furnishings date from 1810 to 1820. Hours: 11 A.M. to 4 P.M. Tuesday to Sunday. Admission: $3 for adults, $2 students and seniors, children under 12 free.

Morris-Jumel Mansion
1765 Jumel Terrace
(West 160th Street)
☎ 212/923-8008

This is the oldest private dwelling still standing in Manhattan. Built in 1765 by Roger Morris, a British colonel, the house was abandoned at the outbreak of the Revolution, and served as headquarters for George Washington in the autumn of 1776. Stephen and Eliza Jumel bought and remodeled the man-

sion in 1810. In 1833, after her husband's death, Eliza married Aaron Burr, then 77 years old. The mansion now is a historic-house museum. The exterior is almost entirely original and is an outstanding example of Federal architecture. There are nine restored rooms, two halls, and a colonial kitchen. The octagonal drawing room has hand-painted Chinese wallpaper and period furniture. Numerous pieces of original Jumel furniture are in the front parlor, where Madame Jumel and Burr were married. Picnic parties are welcome in the rear garden.
Hours: 10 A.M. to 4 P.M. Wednesday to Sunday. Admission: $3 for adults, $2 students and seniors, children under 12 free.

Hamilton Grange National Memorial
287 Convent Avenue
☎ 212/283-5154

This two-story house, on the fringe of Harlem Heights and two blocks from the City College campus, was once the country home of Alexander Hamilton. Born in the Indies, he came to America and fought in the Revolution, becoming an aide-de-camp to Washington. After the war, he studied law and served in Congress, where he helped create the American government. He later served as secretary of the treasury and restored the nation's finances. Hamilton enjoyed his garden here, which he called "a very usual refuge for a disappointed politician." He lived

here only a short time before he was killed in a duel with his political rival Aaron Burr in 1804.
Hours: 9 A.M. to 5 P.M. Wednesdays through Sundays. Admission free.

INWOOD

Dyckman House
4881 Broadway (204th Street–North Amsterdam Avenue)
☎ 212/304-9422

This house, the only Dutch Colonial farmhouse remaining in Manhattan, is now surrounded by supermarkets, apartment buildings, and gas stations, and it's a wonder it survived at all. William Dyckman inherited the farm from his grandfather, who built the first house here in 1748. It was burned by the British in the Revolution and rebuilt in its present form in 1783. In 1915 two descendants purchased the property, restored the house and grounds, and presented them to the city. All the Dutch and English colonial furnishings, clothes, china, and ornaments in the house are authentic. The interior is relatively modest and represents the ordinary style of living in New York at that time. The kitchen with its cauldrons, pothooks, and ovens is the most interesting of the rooms.
Hours: 11 A.M. to 4 P.M. daily except Monday. Suggested donation: $1.

BRONX

Van Courtlandt House Museum
Van Courtlandt Park, Broadway near
242nd Street
☎ 718/543-3344

From 1748 to 1896, this family
estate was a prosperous plantation,
with extensive fields and livestock,
a gristmill and resident community
of craftsmen and field workers,
some of whom were slaves. George
Washington briefly used the mansion as high headquarters, and on
July 21, 1781, dined here with his
French ally Rochambeau prior to
the march from New York to York-
town and the battle that would end
the war. The dining room contains
a portrait of John Jacob Astor by
Gilbert Stuart. The house is furnished with English, Dutch, and
colonial antiques. Hours: 10 A.M. to
3 P.M. Tuesday to Friday, 11 to 4
weekends. Call first to confirm
hours. Admission: $2 for adults,
$1.50 for students and seniors,
children under 12 free.

Wave Hill
West 249th Street and
Independence Avenue
☎ 718/549-2055

Often called the most beautiful
place in New York, Wave Hill is a
28-acre public garden in a spectacular setting overlooking the Hudson River and Palisades. It was
built as a country home in 1843 by
jurist William Lewis Morris. From
1886 to 1903, the estate was owned
by publisher William Henry
Appleton, who brought to Wave
Hill such famous scientists as

Thomas Henry Huxley and Charles
Darwin. Over the years residents
here included Theodore Roosevelt
and Arturo Toscanini. In 1903 the
estate was purchased by George W.
Perkins, a partner of J. P. Morgan
who enhanced the magnificent
grounds. Since 1960 Wave Hill has
been a property of the City of New
York. Visitors can enjoy the extensive grounds, gardens, greenhouses, historic buildings, lawns, and
woodlands. Hours: 9 A.M. to
5:30 P.M. Tuesday through Sunday,
extended hours in summer.
Admission (free Tuesday): $4 for
adults, $2 for students and seniors,
free to children under 12.

Edgar Allan Poe Cottage
2640 Grand Concourse
(East 193rd Street)
☎ 718/881-8900

Poe spent the last years of his life,
from 1846 to 1849, in this small
wooden farmhouse. Built in 1812,
the house once commanded unobstructed vistas of the rolling Bronx
meadows and the shores of Long
Island. Here Poe wrote many of his
most famous works, including
"Annabel Lee," "The Bells," and
"Eureka." He came here in the
hope that it would help his wife's
consumption, but she died shortly
after they arrived. Poe himself died
two years later in Baltimore. The
Bronx County Historical Society
has restored the cottage to its
appearance during Poe's residence,
outfitting it with period furnishings, including the bed in which
Virginia Poe died. Open weekends

only: 10 A.M. to 4 P.M. Saturday, noon to 5 Sunday. Admission: $2.

Valentine-Varian House
3266 Bainbridge Avenue
(208th Street)
☎ 718/881-8900

Set in a park and surrounded by fruit trees and a small colonial garden, this 1758 four-level fieldstone farmhouse was the site of six Revolutionary War skirmishes and was occupied by the British for most of the war. In 1791 the house passed into the hands of the Varian family, who owned it for the next 114 years. In 1965 the house was acquired and restored by the Bronx County Historical Society. It now is the Museum of Bronx History. Hours: 10 A.M. to 4 P.M. Saturdays, 1 to 5 Sundays. Admission: $2.

Bartow-Pell Mansion and Gardens
895 Shore Road North,
Pelham Bay Park
☎ 718/885-1461

This is one of the most beautiful places in all New York. With landscaped grounds, manicured gardens, and a vista of Long Island Sound, the stately mansion reminds visitors of the great homes of Europe. The estate dates from 1654, when Thomas Pell obtained 9,000 acres from the Siwanoy Indians. The original manor house burned, and in 1836 Robert Bartow acquired the property and built the present mansion around 1840. The entry hall, which has an elliptical stairway, leads to the drawing room and the dining room, with windows and doors decorated with carved eagles and winged cherubs. The sitting room, library, and the bedrooms are all superbly furnished. The mansion was restored by the International Garden Club and has been the club's headquarters since 1914. For two summers while he was mayor, Fiorello La Guardia lived here. Hours: noon to 4 P.M. Wednesdays, Saturdays, and Sundays. Admission: adults $2.50, students and seniors $1.25, children under 12 free.

BROOKLYN

The Lefferts Homestead
Boreum Place and Schermerhorn Street
☎ 718/330-8601

In 1776, in anticipation of a British invasion, the Lefferts abandoned the original house here, and it was destroyed during the Battle of Long Island. The Lefferts rebuilt their house in 1777, and today it is a notable example of Dutch Colonial architecture. Like the Dyckman House, it has a steeply pitched gambrel roof, three dormers, and a deep overhang supported by columns. On the first floor are the library, dining room, tea room, and a back bedroom. Furnishings include a 1661 Dutch table, a Hepplewhite sofa, a Pembroke table, and a tall clock. Among the furnishings in the upstairs bedrooms are a quilting frame, a sleigh bed, and several Dutch "playthings of early America." Hours vary according to the season. Admission: $2.

QUEENS

Bowne House
Bowne Street at 37th Avenue,
Flushing
☎ 718/359-0528

This is one of the oldest houses in
New York, built in 1661 by John
Bowne on land purchased from the
Indians. It is also a testimony to
religious freedom. John Bowne
expounded his Quaker philosophy
in violation of Governor Peter
Stuyvesant's edict that the Dutch
Reformed Church be the only reli-
gion. Browne was arrested, impris-
oned, and subsequently banished
to Ireland. However, his coura-
geous commitment and determina-
tion eventually brought freedom of
assembly for the Quakers. A
plaque in the garden commemorates the Flushing Remonstrance,
an appeal dated December 27,
1657, petitioning the governor for
liberty of conscience for the
Quakers. Hours: 2:30 to 4:30 P.M.
Tuesdays, Saturdays and Sundays.
Admission: adults $4, seniors $3,
students $2, children under 12
free.

Kingsland House
143-35 37th Avenue (off Parsons
Boulevard), Flushing
☎ 718/939-0647

This homestead, which is steps
away from the Bowne House, was
built in 1774 by Charles Doughty, a
wealthy Quaker farmer who reput-
edly freed the first slave in Queens.
The architecture is a mixture of the
Dutch and English style once common to the area. The gambrel roof,
central chimney, and quadrant windows are English while the split-
front door and the building's
proportions are Dutch. The house
stands next to the oldest weeping
beech tree in America. Hours: 2:30
to 4:30 P.M. Tuesdays, Saturdays,
and Sundays. Admission: adults
$4, seniors $3, students $2, chil-
dren under 12 free.

King Manor
153rd Street and Jamaica Avenue,
Jamaica
☎ 718/206-0545

The Kings were one of America's
leading families. Rufus King grad-
uated from Harvard in 1777, served
as a delegate to the Continental
Congress, served as minister to
England under Washington,
Adams, and Jefferson, and later
represented New York in the U.S.
Senate. King bought this estate in
1805 for $12,000. For the short
time he lived in the manor, he
enjoyed the life of a gentleman
farmer. At various times the manor
has been an inn, a farmhouse, and
a parsonage for the nearby Grace
Episcopal Church. Unfortunately,
the eight-room house has been
decorated and furnished haphaz-
ardly over the years. Hours: 1 to
4 P.M. Thursdays. Admission:
adults $2, children $1.

STATEN ISLAND

Conference House
7455 Hylan Boulevard
(south end of boulevard)
☎ 718/984-2086

This beautiful house was the site, on September 11, 1776, of the last peace conference between delegates of the Continental Congress and the British government. John Adams, Edward Rutledge, and Benjamin Franklin traveled from Philadelphia to meet with Admiral Lord Howe in a last-ditch effort to avoid war. This house was then called the Billopp Manor House, built around 1680 by Royal Navy Captain Christopher Billopp. His descendants lived here until the war began and the property of all pro-British colonists was confiscated. Restoration of the house began in 1936, and today it looks as it did on the eve of the Revolution. Among the furnishings is a tilt-top table given to John Adams by Lafayette, and an 1850 lithograph showing the house from across the river. This is one of the most beautiful and romantic spots in New York. Hours: 1 to 4 P.M. Friday to Sunday, March through December. Admission: for adults $3, seniors and students $2, children 2 to 12 $1.

Alice Austen House
2 Hylan Boulevard (near Bay Street)
☎ 718/816-4506

This restored house contains work by the remarkable photographer Alice Austen. Her collection of glass negatives, taken between 1880 and 1930, is now held by the Staten Island Historical Society. The house, which has magnificent views of Upper New York Bay, was acquired as a summer home in 1844 by Alice's grandfather, a wealthy New Yorker. He added the Gothic Revival details and peaked dormer windows and named the house "Clear Comfort." When Alice was two, her father deserted the family. Her mother resumed her maiden name and moved into Clear Comfort. Alice lived here until she was seventy-nine, when, ill and destitute, she was forced to move into a city nursing home. A 1951 article in *Life* magazine give her work, at last, the recognition it deserved. Hours: noon to 5 P.M. Thursday through Sunday. Admission: $2.

Garibaldi-Meucci House
420 Tompkins Avenue
(Chestnut Avenue)
☎ 718/442-1608

In 1850 the exiled Italian liberator Giuseppi Garibaldi moved into this frame house, the home of his friend Antonio Meucci. Garibaldi returned to Italy in 1854 and eventually unified the peninsula. Meucci went on to invent a prototype of the telephone years before Alexander Graham Bell produced his. A small museum in the house tells the story of the two remarkable men. Hours: 1 to 5 P.M. Tuesday to Friday, closed on major holidays. Suggested donation: $3.

The Richmondtown Restoration
441 Clark Avenue (near Vanderbilt
Avenue), Richmondtown
☎ 718/351-1611

This is a restored village and
museum complex that interprets
three centuries of daily life in
Staten Island. Located on a 100-
acre site, it includes a 30-acre
exhibition area that contains the
original village center and 27 historical buildings. Many of the
buildings have been relocated from
other Staten Island sites, restored
and furnished with period pieces.
Guided tours of the village buildings are given, along with demonstrations of daily activities of early
Staten Islanders. The complex
includes a restaurant and gift shop.
Hours: 1 to 5 p.m. Wednesday to
Sunday. Admission: adults $4, stu-
dents and seniors $2.50, children
under 12 free.

Déjà Views:
Places to View the City

When the city wears heavy, and you're beginning to think that
the bucolic life is for you, go where you can see the city spread
out before you. Drink it in. Feel the magic. All New Yorkers
have their favorite views. A particularly enjoyable view is seeing
the lights of the East Side from the Queensboro Bridge when
coming from La Guardia Airport at night.

**Empire State Building
Observatories**
350 Fifth Avenue (West 34th Street)
Enter the building on the West 34th
Street side.
☎ 212/736-3100, ext. 73 for the
Observation Deck; 212/564-2224 for
the ticket booth.

On the 86th floor, there is an open
platform on all four sides, protected
with wire mesh and metal bars. A
few steps up is a glass-enclosed
snack bar and souvenir shop. If you
wish to go higher, an elevator will
whisk up to the enclosed 102nd
floor lookout, where the view is just

Above the Statue of Liberty

different enough to be worth the trip. Certainly, it's a tourist attraction, but if you let that stop you, you'll be the loser. Cary Grant waited in vain here for Deborah Kerr in *An Affair to Remember*, and Tom Hanks and Meg Ryan rendezvoused here in *Sleepless in Seattle*. A view has a way of making romantics of us all. On the second floor of the Empire State Building, you can see some of the other sights in the city by taking the seven-minute **Skyride,** a simulated-helicopter sightseeing tour. You'll see the Brooklyn Bridge, the World Trade Center and the roller coaster at

Coney Island. Hours: 9:30 A.M. to midnight daily. A combination ticket ($6 for adults, $3 for seniors and children under 12) includes the Skyride and the Observation Deck.

Brooklyn Heights
Pierrepoint and Montague Streets at the East River

From the promenade you can see the harbor with the Statue of Liberty, the towers of Wall Street, the Brooklyn Bridge, and up the East River. It's particularly lovely by early light and at dusk, when the financial district's lights come on. It's an arguably better view than

The Empire State Building

the one at the River Cafe, and it's free.

World Trade Center
50 Liberty Street
(West Church Street)
☎ 212/323-2340

Purchase a ticket on the mezzanine level at 2 World Trade Center, then take the quarter-mile, 58-second elevator ride to **The Observation Deck.** Floor-to-ceiling windows give you an unobstructed view, and unobtrusive diagrams explain what you're seeing. If the weather is good, take the escalator up to the open rooftop observatory, the tallest

outdoor platform in the world. Hours: 9:30 A.M. to 9:30 P.M. September to May; 9:30 A.M. to 11:30 P.M. June to August. Admission: adults $12.50, students $10.75, seniors $9.50, children 6 to 12 $6.

The Restaurant at Windows on the World offers another version of the view. From the cocktail area you look out at the harbor, and depending upon your table in the dining room, you face north or east. A jacket and tie are required, and so are reservations. Expensive.
1 World Trade Center, Liberty Street (West Church Street) 212/524-7000

New York Harbor, with the twin World Trade Center towers in the background

New York's downtown skyline

On the river, just north of the World Trade Center, is the small **Hudson River Park**, with great views of the Statue of Liberty and Ellis Island. It's a pleasant place to sit and relax, watch people, and think long thoughts.

An unusual view of the city awaits at **Clocktower Gallery,** where many young artists have studio space. From the balcony enjoy the 360-degree view of Broadway, the Hudson, Manhattan Bridge, the World Trade Center, and the Woolworth Building. What makes the view exceptional is that you're not way up high looking down on the city; you're low enough to hear traffic noise. Hours: noon to 6 P.M. Thursday to Saturday. Suggested donation: $5.
108 Leonard Street
(Broadway–Lafayette Street)
☎ 212/233-1096

Across the East River, in Long Island City, savor a great view at the **Public Pier** at 44th Drive. You'll see the ruins of the Smallpox Hospital on Roosevelt Island and the East Side of Manhattan spread out before you.

The **Roosevelt Island Tramway** will take you across the East River's West Channel at 18 mph and along the way give you wonderful views of the East Side and the Queensboro Bridge. Hours: 6 A.M. to 2 A.M. Monday through Thursday and Sunday, 6 A.M. to

3:30 A.M. Friday and Saturday. Fare: $1.50 each way.
Second Avenue
(East 59th–East 60th Streets)
☎ 212/832-4543

Among the many charms of the **Rainbow Room** is a spectacular view of the city. It's best from the bar on the south side. The Rainbow Room is open Tuesday through Sunday for dinner. A jacket and tie are required. Expensive.
30 Rockefeller Plaza
(West 49th–West 50th Streets)
☎ 212/632-5000

A personal favorite is the night view from the art-deco chic of the **Top of the Tower**, certainly one of the most romantic spots in the city. It's in the tower of the Beekman Tower Hotel, at just the right height to enjoy the lights of midtown. Looking east, you can see planes landing and taking off from La Guardia and Kennedy.
3 Mitchell Place
(First Avenue–49th Street)
☎ 212/355-7300

Metropolitan Museum
Fifth Avenue and East 82nd Street
☎ 212/535-7710 or 212/879-5500
The roof garden, open from May to late October, offers great views of Central Park and the city beyond. It is particularly beautiful at dusk when the museum is open late. Hours: 9:30 A.M. to 5:15 P.M. Tuesday to Thursday, 9:30 to 8:45 Friday to Saturday, 9 to 5:15 Sunday. Admission: adults $10, students and seniors $5.

Riverside Church
490 Riverside Drive
(West 121st Street)
☎ 212/870-6700

The tower of this Gothic church, built in 1930 and funded by John D. Rockefeller Jr., rises 21 stories, and its 74-bell carillon is the largest in the world. Visit the Observation Deck in the tower, see the bells, and enjoy the view up and down the Hudson River, from the midtown skyscrapers to the George Washington Bridge. The deck is open from 12:30 to 4 P.M. Sunday.

Another great view of the Hudson awaits at the nearby restaurant **The Terrace**, perched on a Morningside Heights rooftop. The food is best described as French-Eclectic, the view as sublime. Expensive. Reservations are required. The Terrace is open Tuesday through Friday for lunch and dinner, Saturday for dinner only.
400 West 119th Street
(Morningside Heights Drive)
☎ 212/666-9490

Walking Across New York's Bridges

Manhattan is an island of bridges. There are 2,027 bridges serving the city, of which 76 are over water, 329 are used by railroads, 1,011 are over land, and the rest are in parks, subway complexes, or are private pedestrian bridges. There are seven major bridges linking Manhattan to other boroughs and to New Jersey. All seven have pedestrian walkways, a fact not known to many New Yorkers.

On a nice day, it's a joy to walk across the Brooklyn Bridge. To many people, it is still the most beautiful bridge in the world. Along the way, it affords spectacular views of Lower Manhattan, Brooklyn Heights, the East River, and New York Harbor with the Statue of Liberty in the distance.

One of Manhattan's 2,027 bridges

When the bridge opened to great fanfare on May 24, 1883, it was the longest suspension bridge ever built and one of the engineering wonders of the world. The design was the inspiration of John A. Roebling, who had invented the wire rope cables that made the bridge possible, but he died before work got underway. His son, Washington Roebling, took over and completed the project, even though one of his legs had been crushed in a construction accident. His wife, Mary, became his legs, carrying his instructions to the bridge from their Brooklyn Heights home. A plaque on the bridge commemorates her tireless efforts. Soon after the bridge opened, Brooklyn, then a separate city, voted to become part of New York City.

(**Note:** the distances listed combine the bridge spans and the approaches. Unless otherwise noted, all walkways are always open.)

Brooklyn Bridge

☎ 212/442-7033

It spans the East River, from City Hall Park and Frankfort Street in lower Manhattan to Tillary, Washington, and Sands Streets and Cadman Plaza Park in Brooklyn. The walkway is on the upper level in the center of the bridge. The length of the walk is 6,775 feet.

George Washington Bridge

☎ 212/435-7000

Built in 1931, this suspension bridge spans the Hudson River from West 178th Street, just west of Cabrini Boulevard in Washington Heights, to Hudson Terrace in Fort Lee, New Jersey. The south walk is always open. The north walk (179th Street) is closed for construction until 2001. The entire span is 3,500 feet. The length for walkers is about a mile.

Henry Hudson Bridge

☎ 212/360-3000

This 1936 suspension bridge spans the Harlem River at Spuyten Duyvil, from Inwood Hill Park in Manhattan to the Henry Hudson Parkway in Riverdale. The more accessible entrance in Riverdale is at the Parkway off Edsall Avenue near Kappock Street. Only the west side lower pedestrian lane is open. The length of the walk is 2,209 feet.

Macombs Dam Bridge

☎ 212/442-7033

This 1895 swing bridge spans the Harlem River. The north walk starts at West 155th Street and St. Nicholas Avenue; the south walk at Macombs Place in Harlem; both take you to Yankee Stadium in the Bronx. The length of the walk is 2,540 feet.

The Brooklyn Bridge

Queensboro Bridge
☎ 212/442-7033

This 1909 two-level cantilever bridge, also known as the 59th Street Bridge, spans the East River from Second Avenue and 61st Street in Manhattan to Thompson Avenue, 21st Street, Crescent Street, and Queens Plaza in Long Island City, Queens. The north walk and bikeway, at 61st Street, is closed from 2:30 to 7:30 P.M. Mondays through Fridays. The length of the walk is 7,042 feet.

Triborough Bridge
☎ 212/360-3000

This 1936 suspension bridge spans the Harlem and East Rivers from East 125th and Second Avenue in Harlem to Randalls Island. The length of the walk to Randalls Island is 2,593 feet.

Williamsburg Bridge
☎ 212/442-7033

Built in 1903, this suspension bridge spans the East River. In Manhattan the staircase to the walkway is on the corner of Delancey and Ridge Streets on the Lower East Side; in Brooklyn, the entrance is on Broadway and Roebling Street, near South 6th Street. The bridge has a stunning new south walk. The length of the walk is 7,308 feet.

Ahoy, New York!
How to Get Out on the Water

On a warm, sunny day there is no nicer treat than getting out on the water, and New York offers a range of water tour opportunities, from the Staten Island Ferry to a chartered yacht.

South Street Seaport

Circle Line

☎ 212/563-3200

A trip around Manhattan on the Circle has been a New York attraction since the late 1940s. Originally the Circle Line vessels circled Manhattan clockwise, but the direction was later changed to counterclockwise, although no one can remember the reason why. An announcer points out all the sights, recites all the facts and figures, and cracks jokes. The views are so beautiful, you'll fall in love with the city before the boat reaches the Statue of Liberty. Cruises leave from **Pier 83 at West 42nd Street and Twelfth Avenue**; the voyage covers 35 miles and takes about three hours. (The Circle Line also offers various shorter cruises from Pier 16 at the South Street Seaport Museum.) During the summer, there are 12 cruises a day starting at 10:30 A.M. Monday through Friday, 10 per day on weekends. The operation is closed from late December through March. Fee: $22.

Cloud 9

☎ 212/248-3800

This 95-foot yacht can be chartered for weddings and other parties for up to 149 guests.

Great Hudson Sailing Center

☎ 212/741-7245

Sunset cruises on a 43-foot sailboat leave every Friday, Saturday, and Sunday from **Chelsea Pier, on the Hudson River and 23rd Street.** The two-hour cruise with wine and cheese costs $55 and accommodates six people.

Jack's Bait & Tackle

511 City Island Avenue

☎ 718/885-2042

For something a bit less pretentious than the *Honey Fitz*, Jack's will rent you a motorboat seating four for a full day for $50, $65 on weekends ($15 is refunded when the boat is returned).

Lettie G. Howard

☎ 212/748-8590

You can take a retro cruise on this two-masted fishing boat, which was built in 1893. It leaves from the **South Street Seaport** and takes amateur sailors on weekend cruises, sometimes up the Hudson. You sleep in bunks and get meals on Saturday and Sunday. No showers are on board, but facilities are available at marinas along the way. $250 puts you aboard from Friday evening to Sunday afternoon.

New York Water Way Ferry

☎ 800/533-3779

Here are two interesting trips. One is a day cruise to Sleepy Hollow; you go past the Tappan Zee Bridge and take a bus to Philipsburg Manor and Sleepy Hollow. Admission to the historic houses are included in the $38 fare. The other day trip is to Kukuit, the Rockefeller home in Pocantico Hills, for a fare of $60. Both trips leave Saturday and Sunday, May 15 to November 7. The boat leaves from **Pier 78, 38th Street and 12th Avenue**, but if you live in Manhattan a bus will pick you up.

The Petrel
☎ 212/825-1976

This 70-foot former ocean-racing boat holds 36 passengers and goes on a number of cruises during the day and evening, leaving from the **southeast corner of Battery Park**. A 45-minute cruise can be taken during the lunch hour. Prices range from $9 to $26 for evening cruises. The Petrel is also available for charter.

The Pioneer Schooner
☎ 212/748-8786

Built in 1885 and restored several times, this vessel sails from the **South Street Seaport** to tour New York Harbor, going past Ellis, Liberty, and Governor's Islands. Sailings generally depart at 3:30 and 7:20 P.M., but phone to confirm the time. Fare: $20 for adults, $12 for children under 12. On Memorial Day, the Fourth of July, and Labor Day there are evening sails to see fireworks.

Spirit of New York
☎ 212/727-2789 or 212/727-7768

From Pier 62, the Hudson at West 23rd Street, this vessel sails on dinner cruises while the crew performs a Broadway revue. Tickets: Sunday through Thursday $57, Friday $62, Saturday $69.

Staten Island Ferry
☎ 718/390-5253

The distance from the Battery to Staten Island is 6.2 miles, and charter vessels have been making the trip since 1713. Large steamboats were used from 1817 to 1981

The *Spirit of New York*

to accommodate both passengers and vehicles. These were replaced by diesel-powered boats that could carry as many as 6,000 passengers and by a few large vessels for vehicles. As recently as 1990, the Staten Island Ferry was carrying 90,000 people a day.

This trip is an excellent visual orientation to the city. The ferry leaves 24 hours a day from the southern tip of Manhattan, at **South and Whitehall Streets**, weaves through the harbor traffic past the Statue of Liberty and Ellis Island to the northern edge of Staten Island, then returns. Along the way is a glorious view of the skyline. And best of all, the ride is free.

World Yacht Cruises
☎ 212/630-8800

Dinner cruises leave from **Pier 81 (Hudson River and 41st Street)**. A four-course dinner cruise with dancing is $70 weekdays, $85 Saturdays.

Walks into the Past: Historic Tours of the City

The earliest walking tours occurred in the mid-1800s and were excursions into the city's more dangerous areas, particularly the Five Points, around Mulberry Street on the lower East Side. Visiting dignitaries made the tour led by police guides. Charles Dickens took such a tour in 1842 and wrote about it in his *American Notes*. At the end of the nineteenth century the most famous tour guide was a colorful character named Chuck Connors, whose customers included Sir Thomas Lipton and members of the German royal family. Tours today are safe, and even more interesting. Several organizations offer specialized walking tours of the city, and there seems to be a tour for everyone. The Arts and Leisure section of the Friday *Times* carries an up-to-date list of available tours. Here are 11 that caught our fancy:

It's Going to Be a Bumpy Night: A Curmudgeon's-Eye View of the Theater District
☎ 212/629-8813

The tour visits historic theaters, classic movie houses, and television sites from 42nd Street to 57th Street, departing at 10 A.M. Saturday and Sunday. Fee: $10.

Greenwich Village: New York's Left Bank
☎ 212/755-6199

On this tour you can visit the neighborhood that has been home to such writers and artists as Eugene O'Neill, Edna St. Vincent Millay, Edgar Allan Poe, and Edward Hopper. The tour departs at noon Saturday. Fee: $10.

Civil War New York
☎ 212/465-3331

This tour of Lower Manhattan covers sites related to the war, including the sites of the draft riots, a Confederate prison camp, and a house that was a stop on the Underground Railroad. Tours depart at 2:30 P.M. Saturday and Sunday. Fee: $12.

I'll Never Go There Anymore: The Bowery

☎ 212/439-1090

You can tour the area's notorious saloons, dance halls, and flophouses, at 1 P.M. Saturday. Fee: $10, $8 for students and seniors.

Views from the Past

This free tour explores the nineteenth-century history of Central Park, including the Sheep Meadow, the Mall, and the Dairy, every Saturday at 1 P.M. Phone the Central Park Conservatory at **212/935-3960.**

Millionaire's Mile: The Fifth Avenue Gold Coast

☎ 212/935-3960

On this tour you can view the private clubs, palatial homes, and cultural institutions of the area's rich and famous former residents. Fee: $10 adults, $8 students and seniors. Call for schedule.

Greenwich Village Literary Pub Crawl

☎ 212/613-5796

This tour combines readings of works by noted writers with a look at the bars many of them frequented, including the White Horse Tavern, the Cornelia Street Café, and the Cedar Tavern. Among the writers represented are John Steinbeck, Dylan Thomas, Edna St. Vincent Millay, and Jack Kerouac. Tours depart each Saturday at 2 P.M. Fee: $12, $9 for students and seniors.

Grand Central Station

New Delights in the Big Apple

☎ 212/265-2663

The "new" delights on this tour are actually restored old delights, including the renovated Grand Central terminal, the restored Main Reading Room of the New York Public Library, and the new Times Square Information Center. Tours depart at 3 P.M. Saturdays. Fee: $5.

Who's Minding the Store? The History of the City's Great Emporiums and the Merchant Princes Who Built Them

☎ 212/996-1100

Urban historian Jane Marx leads this tour, which includes the histories of Bloomingdale's and Saks. Tours depart at 1 P.M. Sundays. Fee: $20.

Idyllic Island

☎ 212/265-2663

This tour of Roosevelt Island includes the Blackwell House, the Octagon Tower, and a mysterious lighthouse. Fee: $5 and round-trip tramway fare. Call Adventures on a Shoestring for schedule.

Hidden Treasures of Chinatown
☎ 888/377-4455

Both Irving Berlin and Al Jolson started out as singing waiters at the Chatham Cafe, which has been

replaced by the Chinatown Post Office. That's just one stop on this tour, which also visits the eighteenth-century mansion of Edward Mooney in the Bowery. Tours depart at 11 A.M. Saturdays. Fee: $10. Call New York Talks and Walks for schedule.

Touring Behind the Scenes

It's always fun to go backstage to see how things work. These tours and programs will show you the inner workings of some of the city's top attractions.

Metropolitan Opera House Backstage Tour
Lincoln Center, Broadway and 65th Street
☎ 212/769-7020

If you're interested in stagecraft, this tour is a must. You'll see the cavernous backstage area of the Met, where more than 300 artisans design and produce the sets, props, costumes, and wigs that will be seen on stage. The 90-minute tour is given at 3:45 P.M. weekdays and 10 A.M. on Saturdays. Visitors see rehearsal facilities, dressing rooms, and the main stage area. Tours are

conducted by the Metropolitan Opera Guild. Reservations are a must.

Lincoln Center Guided Tour
62nd to 65th Streets at Columbus Avenue
☎ 212/875-5530

This one-hour tour is an introduction to Lincoln Center, an overview of the buildings, the art, the facts and figures. You may be lucky and see part of a rehearsal, or you may be unlucky and find that a building is off the tour because of a performance. Tours are given from

10:30 A.M. to 4:40 P.M. daily. Reservations are advised. Admission for adults is $9.50, students and seniors $8.

Radio City Music Hall Backstage Tours
1250 Avenue of the Americas (51st Street)
☎ 212/632-4041

An interesting one-hour tour of one of the world's great theaters is given daily, depending on the Music Hall's activities. It leaves from the lobby, and visitors are shown the backstage area, the recording studios, the rehearsal hall, the costume rooms, and the technical equipment. Admission is $13.75. Phone for details.

NBC Studio Tour
30 Rockefeller Center (Fifth–Sixth Avenues)
☎ 212/664-4444, ext. 4000

Tours are conducted from 8 A.M. to 7 P.M. daily, with extended hours during the holiday season. Admission for adults is $17.50, seniors and children 6 to 16 $15, children under 6 not admitted.

New Amsterdam Theatre
214 West 42nd Street (Seventh–Eighth Avenues)
☎ 212/262-2900

A backstage tour of the state-of-the-art theater Flo Ziegfeld built for his Follies is conducted hourly from 11 A.M. to 5 P.M. Monday and Tuesday. Price: $10.

Carnegie Hall

Carnegie Hall
West 57th Street at Seventh Avenue
☎ 212/247-7800

One-hour tours of this legendary concert hall are given at 11:30 A.M. and 2 and 3 P.M. Monday, Tuesday, Thursday, and Friday. Admission for adults is $6, students and seniors $5, children under 12 $3.

Grand Central Station
East 42nd Street at Park Avenue
☎ 212/935-3960

Free tours of the newly restored station are given by members of the Municipal Arts Society at 12:30 P.M. Wednesday.

New York Public Library
Fifth Avenue (40th–42nd Streets)
☎ 212/869-8089

Free tours are conducted at 11 A.M. and 2 P.M. Monday to Saturday.

Madison Square Garden
Seventh Avenue (West 31st–West 33rd Streets)
☎ 212/465-5800

One-hour tours of this famous arena are conducted hourly from 10 A.M. to 3 P.M. Monday to Saturday, hourly from 11 to 3 Sunday. Admission is $14 for adults, $12 for children 12 and under.

United Nations
First Avenue at East 45th Street
☎ 212/963-5800

Visitors see the Security Council chamber, the General Assembly room, and historic exhibits on a 45-minute tour. Tours are conducted daily, every half-hour from 9:15 A.M. to 4:45 P.M. Admission is $7.50 for adults, $5.50 for seniors, $4.50 for high school students, $3.50 for children in grades 1–8, children under 5 not admitted.

Metropolitan Museum of Art
Fifth Avenue at East 82nd Street
☎ 212/535-7710

Free highlight tours of the museum's treasures are included in the admission price and are given daily except Monday at 15-minute intervals beginning at 10:15 A.M. Suggested donations: $10 for adults, $5 for children.

American Museum of Natural History
Central Park West and West 79th Street
☎ 212/769-5100

Free highlight tours for visitors are conducted daily at 1:15, 2:15, and 3:15 P.M.

The American Museum of Natural History

Harlem reaches from 110th Street to about 165th Street, and from the Harlem River to Morningside Avenue. Two organizations offer tours of this fascinating area: Harlem Spirituals (212/302-2594) and Harlem Your Way! (212/690-1687).

Gracie Mansion
East End Avenue at East 88th Street
☎ 212/570-6130

Tours of the mayor's residence are given by reservation at 10 A.M., 11 A.M., 1 P.M., and 2 P.M. Wednesday. Admission: $4 for adults, $3 for seniors.

Federal Reserve Bank of New York
33 Liberty Street
(William–Nassau Streets)
☎ 212/720-6130

Free tours of the bank are given hourly from 9:30 A.M. to 2:30 P.M. Monday to Friday.

Fulton Fish Market
85 South Street
(Fulton Street–Beekman Place)
☎ 212/748-8590

A tour of this famous market is given at 6 A.M. weekdays. Admission is $10.

Cathedral of St. John the Divine
Amsterdam Avenue at 112th Street
☎ 212/932-7347

Phone ahead for details of tour and cost.

New York Times
228 West 43rd Street
(Seventh–Eighth Avenues)
☎ 212/566-1234, ext. 4650

Phone ahead for tour details.

Seagram Building
375 Park Avenue
(52nd–53rd Streets)
☎ 212/572-7000

Phone ahead for tour details.

Yankee Stadium
East 161st Street and River Avenue
☎ 718/293-4300, ext. 552

A free tour of The House that Ruth Built is given Monday to Friday during the baseball season. The tour forms at noon at the stadium press gate.

Helicopter Tours

Helicopters are too new to be retro, but a flight in a helicopter can give you a new look at Old New York, and that's what retro is all about. To thrill to the ultimate views of the city is expensive but certainly impressive.

Liberty Helicopter Tours
VIP Heliport, Twelfth Avenue at 104 West Broadway
☎ 212/967-6464

The Liberty copters are larger than most and the ride is smoother. There are 10 to 40 rides a day, depending on the weather. Several tour options are offered, and even the shortest ride is long enough to get a close-up view of the Statue of Liberty and Ellis Island. Tours cost from $46 to $159.

Helicopter Flight Services
1 Penn Plaza, 250 West 34th Street
☎ 212/355-0801

Rides are offered from 10 A.M. to 6 P.M. Monday to Friday, 11 to 6 Saturday and Sunday, and two options are available: New Yorker, 12 to 15 minutes, $99, and the Ultimate Tour, 18 to 21 minutes, $139.

ON THE TOWN

Restaurants Past the Century Mark

In a city that seems to be perpetually changing and considering the high mortality rate in the restaurant business, it is incredible that all of these 19 restaurants have been in business more than a century. And the list would be longer by eight if we counted restaurants in buildings more than a century old. The Old Bermuda in Staten Island, for example, is housed in a mansion that was built in 1716.

Fraunces Tavern (1763)
54 Pearl Street (Broad Street)
☎ 212/269-0144

This handsome Georgian brick building, built in 1719, became Samuel Fraunces's tavern in 1763 and became famous when George Washington said farewell to his officers here on December 4, 1783. Today it serves up American fare to Wall Streeters and tourists alike. The restaurant is open Monday through Friday, for breakfast, lunch, and dinner.

The Ear Inn (1817)
326 Spring Street
(Greenwich–Washington Avenues)
☎ 212/226-9060

When this Irish pub opened, the shoreline was only five feet from the front door, and the trade was mostly rowdy sailors. Today it is the "quintessential New York dive bar" with good pub food and the "strongest margarita in town." The Ear Inn is open daily for lunch, dinner, and late-night snacks.

Pete's Tavern (1864)
129 East 18th Street (Irving Place)
☎ 212/473-7676

At the turn of the twentieth century, O. Henry, a regular patron, used to write short stories in the booth across from the bar. Today it serves up Italian specialties, and has a sidewalk cafe during the summer. Pete's is open daily for lunch and dinner.

Landmark Tavern (1868)
626 11th Avenue
(West 45th–West 46th Streets)
☎ 212/757-8595

This old waterfront tavern has become refined over the years, but hasn't tampered with its nineteenth-century rooms. Food is still served from antique sideboards. Specialties include freshly baked Irish soda bread, prime rib, shepherd's pie, and fish-and-chips. The tavern is open daily for lunch and dinner.

Old Homestead (1868)
56 Ninth Avenue (West 14th Street)
☎ 212/242-9040

From the beginning, steaks and prime rib have been the specialties in this, the oldest steak house in Manhattan. Located in the wholesale meat district, it has a gourmet shop next door where patrons can buy steaks and superb imported chocolates. The restaurant is open daily for lunch and dinner; the gourmet shop Monday through Saturday.

Billy's (1870)
948 First Avenue
(52nd–53rd Streets)
☎ 212/753-1870

If you live on Beekman or Sutton Place, this family-owned place might well be your neighborhood steak house. It serves good, simple American food, and the crowd is mostly regulars. Billy's is open daily for lunch and dinner; it also serves Sunday brunch.

Fanelli Cafe (1872)
94 Prince Street (Mercer Street)
☎ 212/226-9412

When this cafe opened, this was a factory neighborhood, and its patrons were factory workers. It still has a gritty, tavern-like atmosphere. Hamburgers are good; the rest of the offerings are adequate. Inexpensive. No credit cards are accepted. The cafe is open daily for lunch, dinner, and late-night snacks.

Harry's at Hanover Square (1875)
1 Hanover Square
(Pearl–Stone Streets)
☎ 212/425-3412

This has been a Wall Street institution since anyone can remember, and to be on the Street is to have gone to Harry's for closing parties. It's clubby and very male, and the food is Continental. Harry's is open Monday through Friday for lunch and dinner.

Gage & Tollner (1879)
372 Fulton Street (Jay Street),
Brooklyn
☎ 718/875-5181

After years of neglect, this Brooklyn institution has been refurbished, and a new chef has brought the kitchen back up to snuff. Once again it is attracting serious eaters. The restaurant is open daily for lunch and dinner.

White Horse (1880)
567 Hudson Street
(West 11th Street)
☎ 212/243-3956

Many have tried but the poet Dylan Thomas succeeded in drinking himself to death here. Supposedly his last words were, "I've had 19 straight whiskeys. I believe that's the record." The White Horse serves bar food and is open daily from 11 A.M. to 2 A.M. (until 4 A.M. on Sundays).

Keen's Steak House (1885)
72 West 36th Street
(Fifth–Sixth Avenues)
☎ 212/947-3636

From the beginning, Keen's has been famous for mutton chops and for the collection of antique clay pipes, each signed by a patron, which hang from the ceiling. All the dishes are made from old recipes. One almost expects Diamond Jim Brady and Lillie Langtry to be at the next table. Keen's is open for lunch and dinner daily except Sunday.

Peter Luger (1887)
178 Broadway (Driggs Avenue), Williamsburg, Brooklyn
☎ 718/387-7400

Still a top steak house after many years, it has one great specialty—porterhouse steak from prime, aged Iowa corn-fed beef, cooked perfectly to order. Reservations are required. The restaurant is open daily for lunch and dinner.

Katz's Deli (1888)
205 East Houston Street (Ludlow Street)
☎ 212/254-2246

In 1989 this venerable deli was the location for the scene in *When Harry Met Sally* where Meg Ryan faked an orgasm for Billy Crystal. Show business aside, the pastrami is great. Katz's is open daily for breakfast, lunch, and dinner. No credit cards are accepted.

P. J. Clarke's (1890)
915 Third Avenue (55th Street)
☎ 212/759-1650

It seems like only yesterday that Third Avenue had a dozen Irish bars like this, and the El rumbled overhead. And there was a time when you could see Bobby Kennedy or Ari Onassis eating in

the back room. Now it's an institution. The bar has good draft beer and mediocre food. It's worth the trip to see the monstrous urinals in the men's room. P. J. Clarke's is open daily for lunch, dinner, and late-night dining.

Ferrara (1892)
195 Grand Street (Mott–Mulberry Streets)
☎ 212/226-6150

This Little Italy establishment is part cafe, part espresso bar, and part purveyor of pastries and other Italian baked goods. When the weather is nice, there's a sidewalk cafe. Ferrara is open daily.

Hurley's (1892)
1240 Sixth Avenue (49th Street)
☎ 212/765-8981

Somehow this Irish saloon managed to survive when Rockefeller Center was built, and it became the watering hole for the NBC folks who work nearby. It's also popular with theatergoers. The menu revolves around steaks, chops, and burgers. Hurley's is open daily for lunch and dinner.

Old Town Bar (1892)
45 East 18th Street (Park Avenue South–Broadway)
☎ 212/529-6732

After many years, this bar still packs them in, in its time-worn wooden booths, for mugs of draft beer, burgers, and other bar specials. The bar is open daily for lunch, dinner, and late-night meals.

Veniero's Pasticceria & Cafe (1894)
342 East 11th Street
(First–Second Avenues)
☎ 212/674-7070

Old mirrors and chandeliers betray the age of this bakery/cafe, but the customers come here for the biscotti, the cheesecakes, and the pastries. The seating area is usually crowded. No credit cards are accepted. Veniero's is open daily.

Rao's (1896)
455 114th Street (Pleasant Avenue)
☎ 212/722-6709

The eight tables in this East Harlem Italian restaurant are always crowded, the entrees always seem to involve tomato sauce, and the jukebox always plays Sinatra. Rao's is open daily.

 # Ten Romantic Restaurants

Romantic dinners have been working their magic since Eve served the apple in the Garden of Eden, and you can't get any more retro than that. Remember, though, that the restaurant is merely the stage, and the dinner only a prop for the two-character romantic comedy in which you are costarring. If you stumble, forget your lines, or miss your cues, don't depend on champagne or Muscovy duck to pull you through. Of course, if your performance is inspired and Cupid is with you, a bench in Central Park and a bag of peanuts will do the trick. For those of us who need all the help we can get, here are ten of the city's most romantic restaurants.

The Box Tree
250 East 49th Street
(Second–Third Avenues)
☎ 212/758-8320

The walls are glazed dark green, the decor suggests an English country inn, and one reviewer described it as a "charmed, otherworldly experience." The French menu offers such delights as snails in Pernod butter gratinee, filet of beef with cracked coriander and Armagnac, and cocette of raspberries. The fixed-price dinner is exceedingly pricey, but should love conquer all, this is where it will happen.

Cafe des Artistes
1 West 67th Street
(Columbus–Central Park West)
☎ 212/877-3500

Howard Chandler Christie decorated the walls of this intimate bistro with a mural of naked maidens at play in a fantasized woodland. The atmosphere and the food are both delightfully Parisian. President Clinton insisted on dining here when he came to the city. The salmon four ways is a must. Jacket and tie are required after five. This is a perfect place to dine before a concert at Lincoln Center. The weekend brunch is deservedly popular.

Jezebel
640 Ninth Avenue (45th Street)
☎ 212/582-1045

If Tennessee Williams had designed a seductive restaurant in the Theater District, it would probably look just like this. Imagine chandeliers, candlelight, lace, Oriental carpets, and a pianist playing songs of unrequited love. The menu includes shrimp creole, Charleston she-crab, honey chicken, and banana pudding with Grand Marnier. Don't get carried away, though, or you'll miss your curtain.

L'Absinthe
227 East 67th Street
(Second–Third Avenues)
☎ 212/794-4950

If you agree that dark red banquettes, mirrors, flowers, and a Parisian ambiance are very romantic, you'll fall in love with this East Side hideaway. Jean-Michael Bergougnoix, the chef/partner, is inspired, as you'll agree when you taste his lobster salad with black truffle and celery remoulade, roasted duck with chutney and braised endive, and other delights.

La Cote Basque
60 West 55th Street
(Fifth–Sixth Avenues)
☎ 212/688-0666

If all else fails, take your love to one of New York's finest, a restaurant founded by the legendary Henri Soule. There's magic here. The walls are butter-cream, the ceiling beamed with dark wood, and the mural *St. Jean de Luz at La Cote Basque* was somehow moved here from the restaurant's earlier location. The service is impeccable, and the classic French cuisine is superb. Dinner is fixed-price at $62, and lunch is a good value. Reservations are required.

Lutece
249 East 50th Street
(Second–Third Avenues)
☎ 212/752-2225

For more than three decades this restaurant has been rated the finest French restaurant in the city, if not the country. Andre Soltner, the creator, is gone, but his successor Eberhard Mueller is keeping the tradition of excellence intact. The rooms have been renovated in warm Tuscan colors. The flowers in the elegant garden room are spectacular. Some signature dishes remain: truffle with foie gras in croissant, mousse of duckling with

Tavern on the Green

juniper berries, medallions of veal with morels, and frozen raspberry souffle. Expensive. Prix fixe only.

One if by Land, Two if by Sea
17 Barrow Street (West 4th Street–Seventh Avenue South)
☎ 212/228-0822

In an elegant Greenwich Village town house where Aaron Burr once lived, you'll find a working fireplace, red roses on your table, and a pianist playing songs of love and romance. The food is hearty and good: squab with fois gras, beef Wellington, and such. The restaurant serves dinner only, and reservations are required. (There's no sign at the door, but keep hunting; you'll find it.)

Tavern on the Green
West 67th Street at Central Park West
☎ 212/873-3200

This 1870 building on the edge of Central Park is the home of arguably the most beautiful restaurant in the city. On a summer's evening dine in the outdoor garden. The rest of the year enjoy the Crystal Room, with its chandeliers and, from November to May, the twinkling lights in the trees outside. Considering that Tavern on the Green holds 1,500 patrons, the food is quite good. To make it perfect, arrive (or depart) by horse-drawn carriage through the park. Reservations are required.

The River Cafe
1 Water Street
(under the Brooklyn Bridge)
☎ 718/522-5200

If you don't think that a barge tethered to the Brooklyn shore can overwhelm you, come for dinner when the lights are coming on in the Financial District. Everything about this place speaks to the singular wonder of the city. And if you think that great food and a great view are somehow incompatible, you're in for a pleasant surprise. Try the ragout of grilled octopus and Manila clams, the roasted loin of lamb with onion confit, and, of

course, the chocolate marquise Brooklyn Bridge. The fixed-price dinner is $68 and worth every penny.

Windows on the World
One World Trade Center, 107th floor, West Church Street (Liberty–Vesey Streets)
☎ 212/524-7000

The view from this restaurant from atop the World Trade Center is simply indescribable. The main dining room is an open space, decorated in beige and taupe. Chef Michael Lomonaco, recently of the 21 Club, offers such specialties as Muscovy duck with roasted pears, chestnuts, and port wine, grilled venison chops in cabernet sauce with whisky pecan yams, and a double chocolate delirium, which should be illegal. The wine list is arguably the best in town. Expensive.

Top Theater District Restaurants

The Algonquin
59 West 44th Street
(Fifth–Sixth Avenues)
☎ 212/840-6800

As Sardi's is the theatrical restaurant, the Algonquin is the theatrical hotel, and practically every famous actor and actress has stayed here. There are plush chairs

and small tables in the lobby, where you can have a drink before dinner, summoning your waiter by tapping a nickel-plated bell. For dinner choose either the Oak Room or the Rose Room. Both serve good American-French food. The Rose Room, at the end of the lobby, serves an excellent after-theater buffet. The Algonquin is an integral part of the Broadway scene and a lovely reminder of more gentle times. It's closed Sundays and most holidays.

Barbetta
321 West 46th Street
(Eighth–Ninth Avenues)
☎ 212/246-9171

This elegant restaurant is the contessa of Restaurant Row, 46th Street between Eighth and Ninth Avenues, which is chockablock with restaurants. Crystal chandeliers light a beautiful room, and in the summer you can dine in the garden, which has a fountain and statuary. The cuisine is haut Italian—expensive but worth it. The maitre d' is a charmer and will convince you that your arrival has made his day.

Chez Josephine
414 West 42nd Street
(Ninth–Tenth Avenues)
☎ 212/594-1925

Jean-Claude Baker created this charming restaurant named for his adopted mother, the great 1920s star Josephine Baker. Like Ms. Josephine, the place is flamboyant, with red velvet, blue tin ceilings, and shirred window treatments. Jean-Claude is a good host, and the staff is friendly. The menu includes boudin noir with red cabbage, Chinese ravioli with goat cheese, and down-home fried chicken with sweet potato fries. Chez Josephine is an excellent place to dine when you're going to a show on Theater Row.

FireBird
365 West 46th Street
(Eighth–Ninth Avenues)
☎ 212/586-0244

If you're enchanted by the lifestyle of the Russian nobility before the Revolution, this is for you. The decor is marvelous: chandeliers, satin and crystal, Ballets Russes costumes behind glass, family photographs, Russian books bound in leather, the staff dressed by Oleg Cassini. A new chef has made the cuisine authentic—shashlik of marinated lamb, beef stroganoff, charlotte russe, topped-off poached Comice pear with cranberries or lemon tea cake—a feast fit for a czar. Note: At the FireBird Cafe next door, you can sample the cuisine for less and listen to cabaret too.

Frankie & Johnnie's
269 West 45th Street
(Broadway–Eighth Avenue)
☎ 212/997-9494

You climb a narrow, rickety flight of stairs and you seem to come out in the small, noisy kitchen. There's a small bar—where Jason Robards once told off Richard Nixon—and a small, crowded dining room. It looks like a speakeasy, which it was. One comes here for steak, which the waiter slices at the table for you. The appetizers are Jewish—chopped chicken liver with minced onions and chopped egg, matzo-ball soup, and pickled herring. Both the blueberry pie and the chocolate cheesecake are superb.

Joe Allen

326 West 46th Street
(Eighth–Ninth Avenues)
☎ 212/581-6464

This has been a theater hangout for as long as most of us can remember. Housed in a Restaurant Row brownstone, it is charming and unpretentious, and it serves good, simple food at reasonable prices. Many of the patrons are in show business, and chances are good that you'll see a face you recognize. Blackboards at the ends of the dining room serve as menus. There are no gustatory surprises and no financial surprises when the check comes. The restaurant accepts Visa, MasterCard, and cash only.

Orso

332 West 46th Street
(Eighth–Ninth Avenues)
☎ 212/489-7212

This restaurant has been a success since it opened 16 years ago next door to Joe Allen. Reservations are a must, even for lunch. The decor is modern, the service is friendly, and the rustic trattoria fare is delicious. Pizza is a specialty, as are house-cured salmon, fettuccine with wine-roasted chicken breast, grilled salmon in basil sauce, zabaglione, and pumpkin tart.

Sardi's

234 West 44th Street
(Broadway–Eighth Avenue)
☎ 212/221-8440

This venerable restaurant has been part of the Broadway scene for more than 75 years, and it radiates theater nostalgia. This is the place where opening nights were traditionally celebrated, and its red walls are covered with caricatures of actors and actresses who over the years have performed in the theaters nearby. The food is not up to par, but there is hope: A new chef, Patrick Pinon, was brought from France to perk up the menu.

 Fine Restaurants with Pre-Theater Menus

Thrifty New Yorkers know that pre-theater menus enable them to dine in style without taking out a second mortgage on their co-op. Here's a selection of some of the city's best restaurants offering pre-theater menus. A word of caution, however: At the top restaurants the pre-theater menus still command a high price, but a price substantially below that of the a la carte menu.

Aureole

34 East 61st Street
(Madison–Park Avenues)
☎ 212/319-1660

One of the finest and most popular restaurants in the city, Aureole is housed in a chic East Side town house with a garden. Critics note its "culinary perfection."

Cite Grill

120 West 51st Street
(Sixth–Seventh Avenues)
☎ 212/956-7262

This casual art deco watering hole is a bistro version of the excellent upscale steak house Cite at the same West Side location. The scene can get a bit frantic as curtain time nears.

"44" Royalton Hotel

Royalton Hotel, 44 West 44th Street
(Fifth–Sixth Avenues)
☎ 212/944-8844

Here's your chance to dine at the revamped Royalton Hotel's "44" restaurant at a price that won't shock you. Although the staff is a bit intimidating, the food is memorable, and it's only a short walk to your theater.

Four Seasons

99 East 52nd Street
(Lexington–Park Avenues)
☎ 212/754-9494

This stunning restaurant, designed by Philip Johnson, has been a success since the day it opened. The food is superb, the service attentive, and you have your choice of the Grill Room or the Pool Room,

depending on whether you feel powerful or romantic.

Jewel of India

15 West 44th Street
(Fifth–Sixth Avenues)
☎ 212/869-5544

Indian dishes are well prepared and perfectly served in an oasis of serenity. The pre-theater menu makes this a terrific deal.

La Caravelle

Shoreham Hotel, 33 West 55th Street (Fifth–Sixth Avenues)
☎ 212/586-4252

This beautiful French restaurant is on everyone's list of the finest in the city. Chef Cyril Renaud is a master of innovative French dishes, and you're sure to be welcomed warmly and graciously.

Marchi

405 East 58th Street
(First Avenue–Sutton Place)
☎ 212/754-6272

The tony brownstone with a lovely garden that houses this restaurant is a bit far from the Theater District, but you won't find a more romantic place to dine in the city. Chef Wayne Nish's prix fixe menu is a combination of small American dishes, and the service is superb.

Oceana

55 East 54th Street
(Madison–Park Avenues)
☎ 212/759-5941

If you fancy seafood, it doesn't come any better than this. One critic said it was "like dining first-class on the Titanic without that sinking feeling." The restaurant is proof that a seafood restaurant can be truly handsome.

Pierre au Tunnel
250 West 47th Street
(Broadway–Eighth Avenue)
☎ 212/575-1220

This traditional French restaurant has been in the Theater District for nearly 50 years, and its patrons can't be matched for loyalty. The price is right, and your waiter will make sure you don't miss your curtain.

21 Club
21 West 52nd Street
(Fifth–Sixth Avenues)
☎ 212/582-7200

New York's most famous restaurant, this former speakeasy has updated its menu while retaining such specials as the Senegalese soup, Caesar salad, and the "21" burger. The place reeks of power and success.

Eleven Restaurants That Welcome Cigar Smokers

Few activities are more retro than cigar smoking, and few activities have come back into favor with such vigor. Cigars are a symbol of the good life. A fine cigar and a brandy are the perfect finale to a great meal. But what is more frustrating to a cigar smoker than to finish a meal in a good restaurant and then be told he can't light up? A number of restaurants now welcome cigar enthusiasts, and here are some of the finest:

Angelo and Maxie's
233 Park Avenue South
(19th Street)
☎ 212/220-9200

This lower East Side steak house looks the part with a tin ceiling, wood paneling, posters, and an open kitchen. The food is good, and the prices are pleasantly lower than uptown steak houses. The handsome cigar bar is in the back.

Asia de Cuba

Morgans Hotel, 237 Madison
Avenue (37th–38th Streets)
☎ 212/726-7755

This new restaurant in the chic
Morgans Hotel looks like a dream
in white of pre-revolution Havana.
The upstairs lounge was created
with cigar smokers in mind. The
staff, clad in Nehru jackets, will
explain the Sino-Latino fusion
menu, and sharing is suggested on
your first visit. Pricey.

Bar and Books

1020 Lexington Avenue
(73rd Street)
☎ 212/717-3902

889 First Avenue at 50th Street
☎ 212/980-9314

Citispire Center, 156 West 56th
Street (Sixth–Seventh Avenues)
☎ 212/957-9676

636 Hudson Street
☎ 212/229-2642

There are four of these similar but
separately owned cigar lounges,
two on the upper East Side, one on
the West Side, and one in Greenwich Village. Their club-like atmosphere attracts an appropriately
young and classy crowd. These are
good places to meet for drinks and
a smoke, but plan on eating elsewhere.

Bull & Bear

Waldorf-Astoria, 570 Lexington
Avenue (49th Street)
☎ 212/872-4900

For forty years, this has been the
steak house in the Waldorf-Astoria,
and it's one of the most comfortable restaurants in the city. It's
quiet, the tables are large, the service is good, and the drinks are
generous.

City Wine & Cigar Co.

82 Laight Street
(Hudson–Greenwich Streets)
☎ 212/334-2224

Don't let the name mislead you.
This is neither old nor funky;
rather, it is new, the decor is stun-
ningly modern, and there is even a
well-stocked cigar boutique. The
fare is Southern-inspired, excellent
and imaginative. And could a true
cigar aficionado say no to Cuban
cheesecake? Not likely.

Club Macanudo

26 East 63rd Street
(Madison–Park Avenues)
☎ 212/752-8200

With a name like that, this should
be the favorite place of upscale
cigar smokers. It is. Handsomely
decorated with cigar store Indians
and period prints, it offers an
imaginative menu that would succeed anywhere, cigars or no. Club
Macanudo is quiet at lunch, bois-
terous in the early evening. A nice
touch: Patrons store their cigars in
individual humidors.

Delmonico's

56 Beaver Street
(South William Street)
☎ 212/509-1144

Wall Street's most elegant restaurant has been restored to perfection,
and it's worth a cab downtown to
imitate Diamond Jim Brady for a
night. The menu has delights but

no surprises—Dover sole, lobster Newburg, steaks—all preludes to a cigar.

Maloney & Porcelli
37 East 50th Street
(Park–Madison Avenues)
☎ 212/750-2233

This is a big place, and it's decorated with a fine collection of Americana. It's new but feels like it has been around for decades. The menu has old favorites like steak and lobster and such treats as thin-crust pizza, portobello potato pie, and crackling pork shank. The wine list has 40 wines under $40. Cigar smokers feel right at home.

Monkey Bar
Hotel Elysee, 60 East 54th Street
(Madison–Park Avenues)
☎ 212/838-2600

The crowd in this popular playroom sometimes make it difficult to see the whimsical monkey murals in the gorgeous dining room. You'll see more monkeys on the railings, light fixtures, and napkins. (The bar stools, however, look like giant olives.) The fare is excellent, particularly the sea food—

Maine monkfish, yellowfin tuna, and other delights. The whole place feels like a great 1940s supper club.

Smith & Wollensky
210 East 46th Street
(Third Avenue)
☎ 212/753-1530

This retro steak house deserves its four stars. The rooms are handsome and clubby and display such folk artifacts as eagles, decoys, and weather vanes. Steak and lobster reign, complemented by oysters, baked clams, and fine salads. The wine list is exceptional. Expensive.

The Water Club
500 East 30th Street
(on the East River)
☎ 212/683-3333

In fine weather you can dine outside on the upper deck of this enormous barge moored in the East River. The creative American menu includes Maine crab cakes, smoked shrimp, blue crab and andouille sausage, Long Island duck breast, and rack of baby lamb. The prix fixe dinner is a bargain at $28.

Ten Great Bars

Bars, taverns, and saloons—whatever you call them—have been part of the New York scene from the very beginning. Peter Stuyvesant complained in 1648 that every fourth house in the city was a tavern. After the British captured New Amsterdam, English-type taverns were in style, and elaborate painted signs were mounted in front of such establishments as the White Horse, the St. George, and the White Lion. By the 1850s, saloons were serving thousands of Irish and German immigrants. The saloon was regarded as the "poor man's club," an appealing alternative to the lodging house or the tenement. During Prohibition, saloons were replaced by speakeasies, and New Yorkers went right on drinking. With repeal came the return of the neighborhood taverns and the nightclubs.

Bemelmans Bar

Carlyle Hotel, 36 East 76th Street (Madison–Park Avenues)
☎ 215/744-1600

A great spot to rendezvous on upper Madison is this intimate bar in the posh Carlyle Hotel. It seems to have been lifted intact out of an F. Scott Fitzgerald novel. You can sit at the bar or on a red leather banquette. Don't miss the whimsical wallpaper with paintings by Ludwig Bemelmans, the Austrian writer and painter. And note the baby grand piano. If you arrive after 9:30 P.M. someone very good will be playing it.

Bubble Lounge

228 West Broadway (Franklin–White Streets)
☎ 212/431-3433

If you enjoy the combination of cigars and champagne, this TriBeCa bar seems a little bit of heaven. You'll find comfortable sofas and wing-back chairs. Caviar is on the bar menu, and the live jazz is usually good.

Cedar Tavern

82 University Place
(East 11th–East 12th Streets)
☎ 212/929-9089

If you're meeting someone who enjoys contemporary art, note that at this handsome dark bar once stood the likes of Jackson Pollock, Willem de Kooning, Franz Kline, and other giants of abstract expressionism.

Chumley's

85 Bedford Street (Barrow–Grove)
☎ 212/675-4449

This former speakeasy has no sign and is tucked away where it's easy to walk right by it. The clientele is post-collegiate, the cozy atmosphere suggests an American version of a pub, the food is adequate, and it's a pleasant place to while away a few hours in good company.

P. J. Clarke's

915 Third Avenue (55th Street)
☎ 212/355-8857

When the El was rumbling along above Third Avenue, every street corner had an Irish saloon. Now this is the only survivor, a mahogany and cut-glass classic. The stand-up bar is great, and the restaurant in the back room was a favorite of Bobby Kennedy when he lived in New York. It was used as the bar in *The Lost Weekend*, where Ray Milland came to beg for a drink. The elephantine urinals in the men's room should be a national landmark.

Gallagher's Steak House

228 West 52nd Street
(Broadway–Eighth Avenue)
☎ 212/245-5336

This quintessential New York steak house hasn't changed much since it opened in 1927. A poster of the lovely young Ethel Barrymore still hangs over the maitre d's stand, the walls are crowded with nostalgia, and the beef is as good as it gets. The large circular bar is a great place for a drink, whether you're going to the theater or not.

Gramercy Tavern

42 East 20th Street
(Park Avenue South–Broadway)
☎ 212/477-0777

There are several reasons to meet for drinks in this handsome restaurant. The mural-covered front room is a great bar, and while you're there you can sample the goodies from the four-star kitchen. For some of us, it's worth the trip to see the eclectic collection of Americana.

Joe Allen

326 West 46th Street
(Eighth–Ninth Avenues)
☎ 212/581-6464

The bar in this informal restaurant is our favorite place to have a drink in the Theater District. It has brick walls, a blackboard menu, and posters of Broadway flops. It is not touristy, and everyone in the place seems to be involved with the theater. And if you're making a night of it, closing time is three o'clock.

Oak Room

The Plaza, 768 Fifth Avenue
(at Central Park)
☎ 212/546-5330

If you like to drink in a bar that looks like an exclusive men's club, you'll love it here. A mural depicting Central Park is over the bar; the real Central Park may be seen through the window. Should you decide to eat at The Plaza, we suggest the Edwardian Room, not the Oak Room restaurant.

21 Club

21 West 52nd Street
(Fifth–Sixth Avenues)
☎ 212/582-7200

This is arguably the best bar in the city, manned by the best bartenders in the city. It qualifies as a men's bar because it has no stools; male or female, one stands at the bar. Sofas and club chairs in the lobby accommodate those who prefer to imbibe sitting down. The bar and the Grill Room exude excitement, success, and good times to come.

Some Vintage Coffeehouses

Yes, there were coffeehouses before Frasier and Niles arrived, and here are five that have stood the test of time. Not surprisingly, all are either in or near Greenwich Village.

The Peacock Caffe

24 Greenwich Avenue
(6th–7th Streets)
☎ 212-242-9395

This relative newcomer on the coffeehouse scene has only been around since 1944, although it claims to be the first Florentine coffee shop in the city. They do all their own baking, and the Venetian chocolate rum delight and the Florentine apple torte are scrumptious.

Caffe Dante

81 MacDougal Street
(Bleecker–Houston Streets)
☎ 212/982-5275

Founded in 1915, Caffe Dante serves cappuccino and espresso that are first-rate, as are the baked goods.

De Robertis

176 First Avenue
(10th–11th Streets)
☎ 212/674-7137

This East Village coffeehouse has been in this location and owned by the De Robertis family since 1904.

They serve Italian pastries, cakes, and biscotti, all baked on the premises.

Caffe Roma
385 Broome Street
(Mulberry Street)
☎ 212/226-8413

This coffeehouse, established in 1891, is charming, with dark green walls and a pressed-tin ceiling. The cappuccino is the real thing. The rum baba and the ricotta cheesecake are excellent choices.

Veniero's
342 East 11th Street
(First–Second Avenues)
☎ 212/674-7264

Known for the quality and variety of its pastries, Veniero's, established in 1894, supplies other coffeeshops and specialty stores. And their coffee is good, too.

Some Contemporary Coffeehouses

Patisserie Claude
187 West 4th Street
(Sixth–Seventh Avenues)
☎ 212/255-5911

Many say this West Village coffeehouse has the city's best regular coffee, croissants, brioches, tartlets, and quichettes.

Patricia J. Lanciani
414 West 14th Street
(Ninth Avenue)
☎ 212/989-1213

This coffeehouse has excellent pastries and espresso.

DT.UT.
1626 Second Avenue
(84th–85th Streets)
☎ 212/327-1327

The name stands for Downtown-Uptown and it's on the Upper East Side. The chairs are plush, and the coffee and pastries are excellent.

(Opposite) New York at night

High Tea and Where to Sip It

High tea is a delightful custom, a late-afternoon pause for liquid refreshment accompanied by such delights as pastries, finger sandwiches, and scones. It also is the perfect way to keep your appetite in check if you're dining late. Here are some excellent places for high tea:

Lady Mendl's Tea Salon
56 Irving Place (17th–18th Street)
☎ 212/533-4466

The setting is perfect—the Victorian parlor of the Inn at Irving Place—and the five-course tea served on fine china is probably the best in the city. Tea is served Wednesday through Sunday, and reservations are a must.

Felissimo Tea Room
10 West 56th Street
(Fifth–Sixth Avenues)
☎ 212/247-5656

This Japanese-style tea room is located in a chic store in a turn-of-the-century town house. The Afternoon Haiku Tea offers a large selection of teas, which are served with sandwiches, chocolate chip scones, cookies, and chocolates.

Most of the city's top hotels offer high tea. Some of the best: **Waldorf-Astoria** (The Terrace, $20), **The Plaza** (Palm Court, $29), and **The Four Seasons** (lobby, $26).

MUSIC IN THE NIGHT

Come to the Cabaret:
New Places to Hear Old Favorites

From the 1920s to the '50s, the city had great cabarets, places like the Blue Angel, the Little Club, the Embers, and Julius Monk's Upstairs at the Downstairs. One by one they closed their doors and seemed headed for extinction. But new cabarets began springing up to please new generations who stay up late for live comedy or to listen to songs of unrequited love.

Oak Room, Algonquin Hotel
59 West 44th Street
(Fifth–Sixth Avenues)
☎ 212/840-6800

Just past the lobby toward the back is a paneled room where chanteuses hold forth. Performances start at 9 P.M. Tuesday through Thursday, 9 P.M. and 11:30 P.M. Fridays and Saturdays. Music charge: $50; $15 food-drink minimum.

Cafe Carlyle, Carlyle Hotel
35 East 76th Street
(Madison Avenue)
☎ 212/570-7189

Bobby Short playing here has been one of the obligatory experiences in the city for decades now. The only change is that now he plays with his 15-piece band. He sings old favorites and tells show-business anecdotes. The room is beautiful, the service impeccable.

Performances are at 8:45 P.M. and 10:45 P.M. Tuesdays through Saturdays. Cover: $50, no minimum.

Bemelmans Bar, Carlyle Hotel
35 East 76th Street
(Madison Avenue)
☎ 212/570-9189

More intimate than the cafe, this room seems right out of F. Scott Fitzgerald's New York. Sit on a red leather banquette, admire the whimsical wallpaper by Ludwig Bemelmans, and enjoy the music. Of late, Barbara Carroll, pianist and singer, has been doing the honors. Cover: $10. Performances start at 5:45 P.M. and 9:30 P.M.

Cafe Pierre, Hotel Pierre
Fifth Avenue and 61st Street
☎ 212/940-8185

The room resembles a French chateau—gray and pale yellow,

silks, and ceiling murals. The food is classic and expensive, and the service impeccable. If you come after dinner for the cabaret, expect a good singer/pianist. Music is performed from 9 P.M. to midnight Tuesday through Thursday, 8:30 P.M. to 12:30 A.M. Friday and Saturday, 8:30 P.M. to 11:30 P.M. Sunday and Monday. Charge: no cover; $19 minimum.

Delmonico Lounge, Hotel Delmonico
502 Park Avenue (59th Street)
☎ 212/355-2500

This intimate lounge, which opened in 1998, already has built a reputation for booking exceptional chanteuses. The lounge is open nightly; show times vary. Cover: $15 to $25, no minimum.

Danny's Skylight Room
346 West 46th Street
(Eighth–Ninth Avenues)
☎ 212/265-8133

You're bound to find something you enjoy at this cabaret. The "Original New York Improv" alternates with singers, trios, and the jazz group Sol Yaged and Friends. Entertainment is provided Fridays through Sundays. (Piano bar nightly, no cover.) Phone for show times. Cover: $8 to $15; $10 minimum.

Michael's Pub at Bill's Gay Nineties
57 East 54th Street
(Madison–Park Avenues)
☎ 212/758-2272

Now located in a former speakeasy, Michael's Pub continues its tradition of presenting top singers. Julie Wilson has been making her New York home here of late. Shows start at 9 P.M. and 11 P.M. Tuesday to Saturday. Cover: $20 to $25; $15 minimum.

Rainbow & Stars
30 Rockefeller Plaza, 49th Street
(between Fifth and Sixth Avenues)
☎ 212/632-5000

The view is spectacular, the food is good, and the setting is so elegant you half expect Fred and Ginger to dance by your table. Expect to listen to such stars as Steve Ross and Andrea Marcovicci. The room is on the 65th floor of the GE Building, the same floor as the Rainbow Room. Rainbow & Stars has been recently renovated. Shows are performed at 9 and 11 P.M. Tuesday to Saturday. Cover: $35, dinner compulsory at first show.

Le Bar Bat
311 West 57th Street
(Eighth–Ninth Avenues)
☎ 212/307-7228

The decor of this big midtown nightclub/disco/theme bar/restaurant suggests a Gothic cathedral on LSD. If you seek jazz, the vocalists who perform on Sunday night are usually quite good. The food is good, too. If you want to see what's happening on the city's club scene, this is your best bet. Hours: 11 A.M. to 2 A.M. Monday through Thursday, 5:30 P.M. to 4 A.M. Friday through Sunday. Cover charge: Sunday–Wednesday $10, Thursday $15, Friday and Saturday $20. No minimum.

Don't Tell Mama
343 West 48th Street
(Eighth–Ninth Avenues)
☎ 212/757-0788

You won't find peace and quiet in this gay cabaret, but you will find a lot of talent. The pros are inside; the up-and-coming chorus boys and girls are in the lounge. Be sure to catch Steven Brimberg's Barbra Streisand impersonation, "Simply Barbra . . . The Wedding Tour." Phone ahead; hours and show times vary. Cover: $7 to $15, two-drink minimum. Credit cards are not accepted.

Duplex
61 Christopher Street
(Seventh Avenue South)
☎ 212/255-5438

Comedy is king in this "glittery, garish, gloriously tasteless" West Village gay club. A piano is downstairs; camp, comedy, and performance acts are in the Game Room. Phone ahead; hours and performance times vary. Cover: $3 to $12; two-drink minimum at all shows.

Feinstein's at the Regency
Regency Hotel, Park Avenue
at 61st Street
☎ 212/339-4095

This Park Avenue hotel has joined the cabaret scene in a big way, billing itself as "The Nightclub of New York" and giving singer Michael Feinstein, the heir apparent to Bobby Short, a permanent showcase in the city. Other headliners, like Rosemary Clooney, appear from time to time. Dinner shows

The Russian Tea Room

start at 8:30 Tuesday to Saturday, and an additional supper show begins at 11 P.M. Friday and Saturday. Cover: $60.

FireBird Cafe
363 West 46th Street
(Eighth–Ninth Avenues)
☎ 212/586-0244

This is a Theater District version of the Russian Tea Room—velvet settees, Ballets Russes costumes, gilt chandeliers. The food—blinis, sturgeon roe, borscht, and other Russian favorites—-is excellent, and the singers usually explore the great American songbook. Performances begin at 9 P.M. Thursdays, 9 P.M. and 11 P.M. Fridays and Saturdays, 7 P.M. and 9 P.M. Sundays. Cover: $30; two-drink minimum. Dinner is required for the first show Friday through Sunday.

Upstairs at Rose's Turn
55 Grove Street (Seventh Avenue South–Bleecker Street)
☎ 212/366-5438

Comedy alternates with musical revues in this West Village club. Phone ahead; hours and performance times vary. Cover: $5 to $12; two-drink minimum. Credit cards are not accepted.

Judy's
169 Eighth Avenue
(18th–19th Streets)
☎ 212/929-5410

Now relocated to Chelsea, this cozy piano bar has two performance spaces, a good menu and fine performers, including Judy herself. The bar is open nightly.

Sardi's
234 West 44th Street
(Broadway–Eighth Avenue)
☎ 212/221-8440

John Malino's combo plays jazz standards on Fridays. No cover; $12 minimum.

The Supper Club
240 West 47th Street
(Broadway–Eighth Avenue)
☎ 212/921-1940

This big ballroom with a starry ceiling is next door to the Edison Hotel. The club's big band plays swing music for dancing. Singer/pianist Eric Comstock plays show tunes. The Supper Club is open until 4 A.M. Friday and Saturday and offers pre-theater dinner in addition to its regular fare. Cover after 11 P.M.: Friday $20, Saturday $25; $10 food/drink minimum.

Take the A Train: The New Jazz Clubs of Harlem

In the 1920s, a burst of creativity in Harlem forever changed the stereotypical image of the "Negro." Emerging black artists were a living rebuttal to white-supremacy rhetoric and a model of how the downtrodden can give rise to great art. It was the Jazz Age, and fashionable New Yorkers went to Harlem supper clubs to hear Duke Ellington, Fletcher Henderson, and other exponents of the new music. Today New Yorkers are again hearing young, talented musicians playing exciting music in new clubs.

The Apollo
253 West 125th Street (Adam Clayton Powell Jr.–Frederick Douglass Boulevards)
☎ Phone 212/749-5838 to see who is on the program.

Restored in the 1980s, this former vaudeville house is once again a showplace for black music. Budding talents perform on Wednesday, amateur night. (A young Ella Fitzgerald was an early winner.)

Audubon Bar and Grill
3956 Broadway (166th Street)
☎ 212/928-5200

Dance parties start at 10:30 on Thursday, Friday, and Saturday. Cover charge: $5.

Cafe Largo
3387 Broadway (137th Street)
☎ 212/862-8142

Various artists play jazz at 8 P.M. on Monday, Thursday, Friday, and Saturday. Cover: $5.

Cotton Club
666 125th Street (Riverside Drive)
☎ 212/663-7980

Jazz is performed on Friday and Saturday; call for starting times. Swing gets the spotlight at 8 P.M. on Monday and Thursday. Cover: $30 for jazz, with buffet; $15 for swing, no buffet.

Emily's Restaurant and Bar
1325 Fifth Avenue (111th Street)
☎ 212/996-1212

Live jazz is performed at 8 P.M. Thursday. A deejay and dancing are featured at 10 on Friday.

Wednesday is ladies' night, with a deejay and dancing at 7. Cover: $5 on Thursday.

Gishen Cafe
2150 Fifth Avenue (131st Street)
☎ 212/283-7699

Jazz is performed at 9 P.M. on Friday, Saturday, and Sunday. An Ethiopian band plays at 1 A.M. Friday and Saturday. Cover: Jazz $10, Ethiopian $7.

Lenox Lounge
288 Lenox Avenue (125th Street)
☎ 212/427-0253

Jazz is performed at 10 P.M. Monday, at 9 and 10:30 P.M. Friday and Saturday. Gay night is Tuesday, at midnight. Cover: $8, two-drink minimum; free admission on Monday.

Londel's Supper Club
2620 Frederick Douglass Boulevard (Eighth Avenue–140th Street)
☎ 212/234-6114

Jazz is performed at 8 P.M. Wednesday, Friday, and Saturday. Open-mike night is Thursday, at 10. Cover: $5; $10 minimum.

Miss Mamie's Spoonbread Too
336 West 110th Street (Columbus Avenue)
☎ 212-865-6744

Open-mike night is Monday, at 9 P.M. Occasional sing-alongs take place at 9 Saturday. No cover.

Perk's Fine Cuisine
553 Manhattan Avenue (123rd Street)
☎ 212/666-8500

Live calypso is featured at 7 P.M. Monday, rhythm and blues, jazz, and calypso at 7 P.M. Wednesday and Thursday. A deejay is on hand at 10 P.M. Friday and Saturday. Cover: $7 after 10 on Friday and Saturday.

St. Nick's Pub
773 St. Nicholas Avenue (149th Street)
☎ 212/283-9728

Jazz is performed at 9:30 every night except Tuesday. Open jam sessions are featured at 11 p.m. Monday and Thursday. Open-mike night for singers is Wednesday, at 8. Cover: $5 for two, two-drink minimum.

Showman's
375 West 125th Street (St. Nicholas Avenue)
☎ 212/864-8941

Live jazz is performed at 8 P.M., 10 P.M., and midnight Monday through Thursday and at 10 P.M., midnight, and 2 A.M. Friday and Saturday. You can tap-dance on Thursday at all shows. No cover, but a two-drink minimum.

The Sugar Shack
2611 West 139th Street at 2611 Frederick Douglass Boulevard (Eighth Avenue)
☎ 212/491-4422

Jazz is performed at 8 P.M. Saturday. Cover: $5.

Well's Famous Home of Chicken and Waffles

2247 Adam Clayton Powell Jr. Boulevard (Seventh Avenue near 132nd Street)

☎ 212/234-0700

The Harlem Renaissance Big Band plays at 9 P.M. Mondays. A jazz combo gets the spotlight at 9:30 P.M. Friday and Saturday. Cover: Monday, $15 food minimum plus $5 music charge; Friday and Saturday, no cover.

Harlem Jazz Tour

☎ 718/204-5133

(Lauren's Walking Tours) Tours are conducted at 8 P.M. Friday and Monday. Friday tour focuses on Sugar Hill and jazz history; the Monday tour, on modern jazz. Cost: $90, includes dinner and club fees.

Hi-De-Ho Harlem Tour

☎ 212/281-5802

Michael Henry Adams, a Harlem historian, leads this Harlem-at-night tour. It starts with dinner at Miss Mamie's Spoonbread Too and ends at the jam session at St. Nick's Pub. The tour starts at 8 each Monday. Cost: $50, includes dinner.

All That Jazz and the Clubs Where They Play It

Remember Eddie Condon's? Nick's and Jimmy Ryan's? Did you ever go to Birdland to hear Charlie Parker or Lester Young? Those places are long gone. Part of West 52nd Street has been renamed Swing Street, but it doesn't swing anymore. But be of good cheer. Jazz is hardy, and as one club closes another opens. Here are some of the best on the current scene:

Arthur's Tavern

57 Grove Street (Bleecker Street–Seventh Avenue South)

☎ 212/675-6879

It looks like a dive, but the music and the drinks are good. Arthur's presents Dixieland bands and traditional jazz pianists. It's open nightly. There's no cover, but there is a two-drink minimum at the tables. Credit cards are not accepted.

Birdland
315 West 44th Street
(Eighth–Ninth Avenues)
☎ 212/581-3080

This sleek nightclub features the best orchestras and groups available—Chico O'Farrill's smoking Afro-Cuban Jazz Orchestra, for example, and the Gil Evans Orchestra. The club has good acoustics and good sight lines, plus a surprisingly good kitchen. Birdland is open 5 P.M. to midnight Sunday to Thursday, 5 P.M. to 1 A.M. Friday and Saturday. Cover: $15 to $20, $10 minimum.

Blue Note
131 West 3rd Street (Sixth Avenue–Thompson Street)
☎ 212/475-8592

This is a tacky West Village club that describes itself as the "jazz capital of the world." If it isn't, it's not off by much. It certainly books the top performers who don't usually play jazz clubs. Two shows are booked nightly. The club opens at 7 P.M., with shows at 9 and 11:30. The cover charge varies with each band.

Brasserie Americaine
51 West 64th Street (Broadway)
☎ 212/721-3322

On Sunday this pleasant restaurant becomes a "Jazz Bistro" with the Paul Lindemeyer Trio and guest artists playing timeless jazz. No cover. Music is performed from 6:30 P.M. to 9:30 P.M.

Cafe Carlyle, Carlyle Hotel
95 East 76th Street
(Madison Avenue)
☎ 212/570-7189

On Monday nights, Woody Allen plays traditional Dixeland music on his Albert clarinet with Eddy Davis and His New Orleans Jazz Band. Sets start at 8:45 P.M. and 10:45 P.M. Cover charge: $50; $25 for Davis's late non-Woody set. No minimum.

Deanna's
107 Rivington Street
(Ludlow–Essex Streets)
☎ 212/420-2258

This restaurant with jazz has reappeared downtown. Jazz is played from 7 P.M. to midnight Tuesday through Sunday. $5 cover.

Dharma
174 Orchard Street
(Houston–Stanton Street)
☎ 212/780-0313

This elegant new club offers funky bop and experimental jazz nightly. Happy hour is from 6 to 9. Sets are at 10, 11:30, and 1 A.M.

Fez
380 Lafayette Street
(Great Jones Street)
☎ 212/533-7000

Suffice it to say that the Mingus Big Band plays here every Thursday. Fez also offers dining. It opens at 8:30, with sets at 9:30 and 11:30. Cover charge: $18.

Five and Ten No Exaggeration
77 Greene Street
(Spring–Broome Streets)
☎ 212/925-7514

This will remind you of a some-what tattered '40s supper club. The atmosphere is warm, the music hot. The club opens at 8 P.M. Tuesday to Sunday. $5 cover, $10 food or drink minimum.

Iridium
48 West 63rd Street (across from Lincoln Center, between Columbus Avenue and Broadway)
☎ 212/582-2121

The interior has been described as psychedelic and "neo-Dali." The jazz, though, is authentic neo-conservative, and you'll hear artists a step or two from the big time. A good restaurant is on the first floor, and the music room is downstairs. Iridium is open nightly, from 8:30 to midnight or 2 A.M. The cover charge varies with performers.

Jazz at Noon
San Martin Restaurant, 143 East 49th Street (Lexington–Third Avenues)
☎ 212/832-0888

Unbelievably, this Friday-afternoon jam session is now in its 33rd sea-son. Such giants as Clark Terry and Elvin Jones occasionally stop by and join the first-rate house band. Cover charge: $5.

The Jazz Standard
116 East 27th Street
(Park–Lexington Avenues)
☎ 212/576-2232

Remember hard bop? It's alive and it's here. The club's sound system

is excellent, and the club menu is the best in the city. Sets start at 8 and 10 Wednesday and Thursday, 8, 10:30, and midnight Friday and Saturday, 7 and 9:30 Sunday. Guitarist David O'Rourke swings in the upstairs bar. Cover: $15 to $25, $10 minimum.

Knickerbocker Bar & Grill
33 University Place (9th Street)
☎ 212/228-8490

Some of the finest jazz piano any-where is played in this handsome Village restaurant. The collection of prints and posters is also outstand-ing. Two-drink minimum at bar.

Knitting Factory
744 Leonard Street
(Broadway–Church Street)
☎ 212/219-3055

This club has a wide reputation for presenting the best in avant-garde jazz. The cover charge and set times vary with the performers.

Red Blazer Hideaway
32 West 37th Street
(Fifth–Sixth Avenues)
☎ 212/947-6428

This long-time mecca for those who love swing and Dixieland jazz has found a new home. The club is open nightly. Cover charge: $10; two-drink minimum.

Savoy Lounge
335 West 41st Street
(Eighth–Ninth Avenues)
☎ 212/947-5255

If you enjoyed the ambiance of the old jazz clubs, you'll enjoy this scruffy club, which is near the rear entrance of the Port Authority bus terminal. The music is hard bop and swing blues. Between sets you'll hear a great jazz jukebox. Music is played nightly, starting at 10, 11:30, and 1 A.M. The cover varies with the artists. Two-drink minimum at tables. No food.

Small's
183 West 10th Street
(Seventh Avenue South)
☎ 212/929-7565

Named for a legendary Harlem jazz club, this cozy Village club is open all night. Shows in the candlelit basement start at 10 P.M., the nightly jam around 2 A.M., and things keep going until 8 the next morning. The club is right around the corner from the Village Vanguard. No cover.

Sweet Basil
88 Seventh Avenue
(Grove–Bleecker Streets)
☎ 212/242-1785

A Village favorite, Sweet Basil is an intimate club with good jazz and good food. It's open nightly except Sunday. Sets start at 9 and 11, plus at 12:30 A.M. Friday and Saturday. A jazz brunch is served Saturday from 2 to 6 P.M. The cover charge varies with the artist.

Swing 46
349 West 46th Street
(Eighth–Ninth Avenues)
☎ 212/242-9554

This new club on Restaurant Row bills itself as "New York's only all swing all time jazz and supper club." If the lindy and Charleston

are not in your dance repertoire, lessons are given at 7 and 9 nightly. The music begins at 10. The cover varies with the artist.

Tonic
107 Norfolk Street
(Delancey–Rivington Streets)
☎ 212/358-7501

If you enjoy the Knitting Factory, you'll find similar avant-garde jazz here. Tonic is open Tuesday to Sunday, with sets at 8, 10, and on weekends, midnight. Credit cards are not accepted. The cover charge varies with the performer.

Village Vanguard
178 Seventh Avenue South
(11th Street)
☎ 212/255-4037

This club has seen a lot of jazz history, and is revered by fans around the world. Artists who play here have arrived. The club is open Monday through Saturday. Sets start at 9:30 and 11:30, with a 1 A.M. set on Friday and Saturday. Cover: $15 to $20; $10 minimum.

Zinno
126 West 13th Street
(Sixth–Seventh Avenues)
☎ 212/924-5182

Enough top-flight jazz artists play in this Italian restaurant in the Village to make it a serious jazz club. Music is performed from 8 to midnight. The cover varies with the artist.

Just for Laughs: The Comedy Clubs

Remember when Shelly Berman, Mort Sahl, Phyllis Diller, Woody Allen, and all the other comics were appearing regularly in comedy clubs? Times have changed, but new comedy clubs are the places to see a new generation of talent. Here are the top clubs in the city:

Boston Comedy Club
82 West 3rd Street
(Thompson–Sullivan Streets)
☎ 212/477-1000

Sometimes it gets a little rowdy in this basement room, but you'll see a lot of young comedians perform. On Saturday night the first show is a showcase for new talent. The club is open nightly, with shows at 9:30 weekdays, 8, 10, and midnight on weekends. Times may vary with the performers; phone first. Cover: $5 Sunday to Thursday, $10 weekends.

Caroline's Comedy Club
1626 Broadway
(49th–50th Streets)
☎ 212/956-0191

In Times Square near the Ed Sullivan Theater, where David Letterman holds forth, Caroline's presents both big names and those who may be tomorrow's stars. It all happens in a big, elegant basement—a basement that resembles a TV studio. Monday is "New Talent Night," hosted by Eddie

Brill. Wednesday is "Gemini Lounge," with the Sklar Brothers. Shows start at 10 weekdays, at 8, 10:30, and 12:30 on weekends. Times vary with the performers; phone first. Cover charge: $12 to $21, with a two-drink minimum.

Comedy Cellar
117 MacDougal Street
(Third Avenue–Bleecker Street)
☎ 212/254-3480

It looks like a Greenwich Village coffeehouse in the '60s, and showcases many of the city's top comics. Shows start at 8:30, 10:15, and midnight on weekends, at 9 Sunday through Thursday. Times often vary with the performers; phone first. Cover: $12 and a two-drink minimum.

Comic Strip
1568 Second Avenue
(81st–82nd Streets)
☎ 212/861-9386

All comedy clubs have dull nights, but no one seems to remember a dull night here. An eclectic mix of comedians is presented every night of the week. Shows start at 8:30 and 10:30 on weeknights, 8:30, 10:30, and 12:30 on weekends. Times vary with performers; phone first.

Dangerfield's
1118 First Avenue
(61st–62nd Streets)
☎ 212/593-1650

This Vegas-style club was founded by Rodney Dangerfield 20 years ago, and it's still one of the best. Shows start at 9 and 11:15 P.M. Friday, 8, 10:30, and 12:30 A.M. Saturday, and continuous from 8:45 Sunday to Thursday. Cover: $15 Friday and Saturday, $12.50 Sunday through Thursday.

Gotham Comedy Club
34 West 22nd Street
(Fifth–Sixth Avenues)
☎ 212/367-9000

This big, handsome, trendy club in the Flatiron District is building a solid reputation. Shows start at 8:30 Sunday to Thursday, 8:30 and 10:30 Friday and Saturday. The cover charge is $12 Friday and Saturday, $8 on weeknights; two-drink minimum.

New York Comedy Club
241 East 24th Street
(Second–Third Avenues)
☎ 212/696-5233

A lot of up-and-coming talent appears in this new club. Shows start at 9:15 weeknights, at 7, 9, and 11 weekends. Times may vary with performers; phone first. Cover: $5 from Monday to Thursday, $10 Friday, Saturday, and Sunday.

The Original Improv
241 East 24th Street
(Ninth–Tenth Avenues)
☎ 212/279-3446

The old club is in a new location but still presenting both big names and talented newcomers. As the name suggests, most performances are improvisational. Shows start at 9 Sunday through Thursday, at 7, 9, and midnight Friday. Cover: $10 and $9 minimum.

Stand-Up N.Y.
236 West 78th Street (Broadway)
☎ 212/595-0850

Robin Williams sometimes drops by here to warm up for his Letterman appearances. Shows start at 9 Sunday through Thursday, 7 and 9 Friday, 7, 9, and 11:30 Saturday. The cover is $7 to $12 and a two-drink minimum.

Soothing Sounds: Where to Listen to Chamber Music

The Dutch sang psalms in their own language long after the English captured the colony in 1864. Musical life in the city, though, was undistinguished in the 1700s. The earliest public concert, held in 1712, was advertised as a "concert of musick, vocal and instrumental." The first concert hall was the Nassau Street Theater, where operas were staged from about 1750. Music developed in New York with great rapidity during the 1800s, as immigrants arrived from countries with a strong musical heritage. A popular place to hear concerts was Niblo's Garden at Broadway and Prince Street. Italian opera established a stronghold at the Richmond Hill Theatre at Charlton and Varick Streets. By the mid-nineteenth century, New York was considered the national musical capital, a position it holds today.

In a noisy world, few sounds are more soothing than chamber music. Happily, the city offers opportunities to hear fine chamber music throughout the year—if you know where to look, or, rather, listen. Here is a roundup of the usual suspects:

Bargemusic
☎ 718/624-4061

The Fulton Ferry Landing in Brooklyn is arguably the best place for chamber music in New York. On a barge tied to the landing, you can hear first-rate classical music twice a week with a backdrop of spectacular views of Manhattan. Artists come from all over to play here, and the musical quality is exceptional. Before the concert and during intermission, volunteers serve snacks. From time to time Bargemusic offers candlelight dinners, cooked by volunteers; the events include cocktails, supper, a concert, and dessert at intermission. The cost is $75, with $50 going as a tax-deductible contribution to Bargemusic. Admission to regular concerts is $23 for adults, $20 for students and seniors.

Banjos, Dulcimers, and Such

If you seek the pleasures of folk music, Folk Fone will tell you what singers and groups are playing where and when. 212/674-2508

The Cloisters

Fort Tryon Park (West 193rd Street and Fort Washington Avenue)
☎ For information on programs or to reserve tickets, call 923-3700.

In the magnificent Fuentituena Chapel, you can hear the medieval music that was the forerunner to chamber music, and see morality plays and mystery plays. The performances are held one or two Sundays a month. The Christmas program by the Waverly Consort is particularly popular. The chapel seats 265 and sells out quickly.

The Frick Collection

1 East 70th Street (Fifth Avenue)
☎ 212/288-0700

String quartets, pianists, and small vocal ensembles perform here one or two Sundays each month. The free concerts are held in the 200-seat round music room, which has patterned velvet walls, a skylight, panel paintings by Fragonard, and marvelous acoustics. When the guards close the sliding doors, listeners feel they are in a world of their own. To get tickets, you must mail the Frick a written request, including an SASE, and it must arrive at the Frick before the third Monday prior to the concert.

The Juilliard School

60 Lincoln Center Plaza
(West 65th Street–Broadway)
☎ 212/769-7406

Student and faculty concerts are held several times a week during the school term. Concerts are free, but some require tickets, which can be obtained at the Juilliard box office, up to two weeks before the performance.

The Chamber Music Society of Lincoln Center performs a full schedule of programs each season at Alice Tully Recital Hall, the best and most intimate of the auditoriums at Lincoln Center. Offerings include sophisticated thematic concerts, symposiums, and lectures. Ticket prices are around $35.
1941 Broadway (West 66th Street)
☎ 212/875-5788

Merkin Concert Hall

129 West 67th Street
(Broadway–West End Avenues)
For program and ticket information, phone Centercharge,
☎ 212/721-6500

Near Lincoln Center but not part of it, this small auditorium attracts a knowledgeable audience with imaginative programming, good acoustics, and modest ticket prices.

Metropolitan Museum of Art
Fifth Avenue and East 82nd Street. For a schedule of events or ticket information, phone ☎ 212/535-1633.

Most of the concerts here are held the 708-seat Grace Rainey Rogers Auditorium, usually in series and sometimes thematic. The "Speaking of Music" series, on Saturday afternoons, offers such musicians as the Juilliard and Guarneri String Quartets.

Miller Theater at Columbia University
116th Street and Broadway. For program and ticket information, phone ☎ 212/854-7799.

This theater has won the Chamber Music America/ASCAP Award for Adventurous Programming; the more musically knowledgeable you are, the more you'll enjoy coming here.

Celeste Bartos Forum at the New York Public Library
Fifth Avenue at East 40th Street ☎ 212/930-0571

Three musical events are held here each year, and they are part concert, part reading, and part music-appreciation. A pianist gives a demonstration before each piece. The concerts, the brainchild of hostess Eugenia Zuckerman, are excellent and deservedly popular. Tickets are $8.50 and can be purchased by mail from the Public Library Education Department or in person at the Library Shop.

Nicholas Roerich Museum
319 West 107th Street (Broadway–Riverside Drive) ☎ 212/864-7752

This small museum offers free concerts at 5 P.M. most Sundays. The second-floor music room resembles a cultured home in Eastern Europe, and many of the musicians come from the New York Philharmonic.

Other Places to Enjoy an Opera

The first great opera house in New York was the Academy of Music on 14th Street at Irving Place, which seated 4,600 people. It opened in 1854 with Bellini's *Norma*. In 1906 Oscar Hammerstein opened the Manhattan Opera House, also on 14th Street, where stars like Mary Garden and John McCormick performed. The Metropolitan Opera was built in 1881 at Broadway and 39th Street, financed by a number of wealthy New Yorkers who were unable to obtain boxes at the Academy of Music. It soon became the city's premier opera company, a position it continued to hold after it moved to Lincoln Center in 1966.

Not surprisingly, when New Yorkers think of opera today, most think of the Met, which is one of the great opera companies in the world. They don't realize that the city has a number of small opera companies that provide performers with valuable stage experience on their way up. These companies also give opera lovers the opportunity to hear opera for a fraction of the cost the Met commands. Here's a sampling of these companies:

The Amato Opera
319 Bowery
(First–Second Avenues)
☎ 212/228-8200

Since 1948, this company has presented five fully staged performances a year, drawing primarily from the Italian repertoire, all with clever costumes and sets. They do without an orchestra, using only a piano and a few other instruments. Tickets are $23.

American Opera Projects
463 Broome Street
(Greene–Mercer Streets)
☎ 212/431-8102

Developing American operas by "established composers and people working in other genres" is the mission of this company. It sponsors workshops, outdoor public performances, showcase performances, and back-to-back performances during the Soho Festival in

October. Productions are staged without costumes and sets.

The Bronx Opera Company
5 Minerva Place
(Jerome Avenue), Bronx
☎ 718/365-4209

Under the direction of Michael Spierman, the company, founded in 1967, mounts two productions each year, always in English, and staged at the new performing-arts center at Hostos Community College (Grand Concourse and 149th Street) and at John Jay College (59th Street and 10th Avenue). Each January, the company performs a rare work and, in May, a well-known work.

The Dicapo Opera Theatre
184 East 76th Street
(Lexington–Third Avenues)
☎ 212/288-9438

Four full productions are mounted each year in the 208-seat theater designed and built for the company in the lower level of the St. Jean Baptiste Church. Michael Capasso and Diane Martindale are the skilled directors.

GETTING PHYSICAL

Tennis, Anyone?
Finding a Court in the City

Tennis was introduced to the United States by Mary Outerbridge, who in the late 1870s oversaw the construction of the first lawn tennis court at the Staten Island Cricket and Baseball Club. The first courts in Manhattan opened in Central Park in 1881. If you want to join the fun, you can choose from the bargain public courts or private clubs that range in price from reasonable to mind-boggling. So put on your whites and head for one of the many courts in the city.

Public Courts

You can purchase a $50 permit and play on any of the 908 public courts in Manhattan. Thirty of these are in Central Park (93rd–West River Drive), ten more at Riverside Park, at 96th Street. Twelve courts are at East River Park, near Delancey; ten at Fort Washington Park (Henry Hudson Parkway–172nd Street); nine at Inwood Hill Park (172nd Street); eight at Frederick Johnson Playground at 151st Street (Seventh Avenue), and eleven on Randalls Island. City courts are open from April to November; permits go on sale at the end of March, and are obtained at the **Arsenal**, Fifth Avenue and 64th Street, 212/360-8131, and at **Paragon Sporting Goods**, 867 Broadway (17th–18th Streets), 212/255-8036.

NY Health and Racquet Tennis and Yacht Club

Wall Street Piers 13 and 14
☎ 212/422-9300

This is the place to play if you work on Wall Street. It has eight indoor Har-Tru courts under a bubble. The club gives lessons, arranges games, and holds tournaments. After a $500 initiation fee, a membership is $795 a year, and the courts command $25 to $60 per hour ($50 to $120 for non-members). But if you work on Wall Street, these prices should not trouble you. The club is open daily from 6 A.M. to midnight.

Inside the New York Stock Exchange

**NY Health and Racquet Village
Tennis Court**
110 University Place
(12th–13th Streets)
☎ 212/989-2300

Two Supreme courts and a practice court with a ball machine are on a rooftop under a bubble. Yearly membership is $294. The hourly charge is $31 to $83. There's no initiation fee. Various membership packages are available, some of which include the use of a health club. Hours: 7 A.M. to 11 P.M. daily.

Manhattan Plaza Racquet Club
450 West 43rd Street
(Ninth–Tenth Avenues)
☎ 212/594-0554

The five hard-surface courts at this first-rate club are outdoor from May to September and under a bubble the rest of the year. The initiation fee is $250, the annual dues $750. Hourly rates for members are $28 to $50. You'll probably have to book court time a week in advance. Hours: 6 A.M. to midnight weekdays daily.

Crosstown Tennis
14 West 31st Street
(Fifth Avenue–Broadway)
☎ 212/947-5780

To play on the four indoor Deco-turf II courts here costs $38 to $95 an hour, depending on the season and the day of the week. Rates for 38 weeks, $1,300 to $3,249. Lessons: $80, which includes court. There's no initiation or guest fee. Hours: 6 A.M. to 10 P.M. Sunday through Friday, 6 A.M. to 8 P.M. Saturday.

Midtown Tennis Club
341 Eighth Avenue
(26th–27th Streets)
☎ 212/989-8572

During the winter the eight outdoor Har-Tru courts here are covered by a bubble. The four indoor
courts are air-conditioned. Hourly
rates: $35 to $70. Seasonal rates for
early October to early May: $1,085
to $2,170. The club has lessons,
clinics, leagues, a children's program, and social events. Hours:
7 A.M. to 8 P.M. weekdays, 8 A.M. to
midnight weekends.

Sutton East Tennis Court
488 East 60th Street
(Sutton Place–York Avenue)
☎ 212/751-3452

In a bubble under the 59th Street
Bridge are eight clay courts. The
28-week season, October to April,
costs from $1,176 to $2,912.
Hourly charges: $32 to $104. The
club gives lessons, arranges games,
and holds tournaments and tennis
parties. Hours: 7 A.M. to midnight
daily.

The Tennis Club at Grand Central
15 Vanderbilt Avenue
(42nd–43rd Streets)
☎ 212/687-3841

Prices are high, and amenities are
few, but there is a certain cache to
playing tennis in the station. The
club has two Decoturf courts.
Many time periods are booked for
the season. Seasonal rates are
$1,100 to $2,750; annual rate,
$3,850; hourly rates, $65 to $75.
Hours: 7 A.M. to 10 P.M. weekdays,

8 A.M. to 5 P.M. weekends during the
winter; closed summer weekends.

UN Plaza–Park Hyatt Health Club
First Avenue and 44th Street
☎ 212/702-5016

To play on the one indoor Supreme
surface costs $2,860 for 52 one-
hour sessions. Hourly rates: $55 to
$60. The pool, exercise room, and
the stunning view over the United
Nations and the East River are free
to members. The club is in the
hotel.

Town Tennis Member Club
430 East 56th Street
(Sutton Place–First Avenue)
☎ 212/752-4059

Two of the three Decoturf II outdoor courts are lit for night play.
Members practice on a three-
quarter court with a backboard.
Initiation fee: seniors (40 and over)
$3,000; intermediates (under 40)
$2,000; non-residents $1,100.
Annual dues: $3,350 for seniors
and intermediates over 30, $2,700
for intermediates under 30; $1,150
for nonresidents. $25 fee for sin-
gles per court per hour. To join you
must be recommended by a member and provide a bank reference.
Hours: 8 A.M. to 10 P.M. daily.

The Vertical Club
330 East 61st Street
(First–Second Avenues)
☎ 212/355-5100

This top spa has six indoor and two
outdoor Supreme courts on the
roof. Dues are $2,000 for the first
year, $1,000 in subsequent years,

and include all the other facilities here. Hourly court fees: $20 to $25 additional. The club offers lessons, game arranging, tournaments, and social events. Hours: 6 A.M. to 10 P.M. daily.

Columbia Tennis Club
795 Columbus Avenue (97th Street)
☎ 212/663-6900

The nine Har-Tru courts here are lighted for nighttime playing. Memberships: Individual, $1,750; individual, weekdays only, $1,400. No additional charge for court time. The club will arrange games. Hours: 7 A.M. to 9 P.M. daily.

Trinity Tennis Club
101 West 91st Street
(Columbus–Amsterdam Avenues)
☎ 212/873-1650

The Trinity School rents time on two courts, an indoor with Ball-tex carpeting, the outdoor with Ball-tex mesh. The 35-week season runs from mid-September to mid-May, and costs from $660 to $1,440. Players rent the same hour each week. Hours: 7 A.M. to midnight, except during school hours.

Shove Off, Sailor: Learn to Sail, Rent a Boat

On weekends from April to October, you can learn to sail at the Great Hudson Sailing Center, at the Chelsea Pier, 23rd Street and the Hudson River. The lessons are broken down into four four-hour sessions over two consecutive weekends, and cost $400. (Private lessons are available for $65 an hour.) 212/741-7245

The Hayden Planetarium, at Central Park West and 81st Street, teaches Navigation in Coastal Waters and Beginning and Advanced Celestial Navigation in the fall and spring. 212/769-5900

Tower Tennis Club

East River Tower, 1725 York Avenue
(90th Street)

☎ 212/860-2464

Members play on two Decoturf II
courts, which are covered by a bubble in the winter. Winter rates:
$1,000 to $2,900, or $60 to $80
an hour should there be a cancella-
tion. Lessons are available. There's
little summer play because the
courts, which are in an apartment
building, are not air-conditioned
Hours: 6 P.M. to 10 P.M. Tuesday to
Thursday in summer, 7 A.M. to
midnight daily in winter.

East River Tennis Club

44-02 Vernon Boulevard
(44th Avenue), Queens

☎ 718/937-2381

This Queens facility has twenty
Har-Tru outdoor courts, eighteen
of which are covered with a bubble
in the winter. Rates: $1,750 and up
plus $23 for singles. Amenities
include a pool, limited shuttle bus
service from 57th Street and Third
Avenue, and a great view of
Manhattan. Hours: 7:30 A.M. to
10 P.M. daily.

Tennisport

51-24 Second Street (Borden
Avenue), Long Island City

☎ 718/392-1880

This large facility has thirteen Har-
Tru outdoor courts and sixteen
indoor clay courts. The annual fee

is $2,800 ($1,400 off-peak), plus
$15 per hour during peak periods
and $12 off-peak. Members under
35: $800 a year (non-peak periods
only) and $10 per hour court time.
Lessons and game-arranging are
available. Hours: 7:30 A.M. to
10 P.M. daily.

Roosevelt Island Racquet Club

281 Main Street, Roosevelt Island

☎ 212/935-0250

Twelve clay courts in an air-
conditioned bubble are available
to members. Memberships are
$750 a year with a $500 initiation
fee (less for Roosevelt Island residents). Hourly rates: $24 to $40.
Hours: 6 A.M. to midnight daily.

USTA National Tennis Center

Corona Park in Flushing Meadows,
Queens

☎ 718/760-6200

This world-class facility has twenty-
two outdoor Decoturf II courts, all
lit for night play, and nine indoor
Decoturf courts. Indoor weekday
32-week one-hour memberships
range from $896 to $1,280, with
$28 to $40 hourly rates. Indoor
rates are reduced from mid-May to
October. Hours: 7:30 A.M. to midnight. The Center is open every day
except Thanksgiving, Christmas,
New Year's Day, and when hosting
the U.S. Open in August/September.

Help for Energetic Insomniacs

If you can't sleep or if you wake up early, don't worry. There are a number of ways to pass the wee hours in the city. Some are entertaining, some healthy, some are both.

You can see what happens to people who get into trouble. **Night Court** is in session all night, Wednesday through Friday.
Criminal Court, 100 Centre Street
☎ 212/374-5880

Several pool halls are open around the clock:
Chelsea Billiards
54 West 21st Street
☎ 212/989-0096

Mammoth Billiards, two locations:
114 West 26th Street
☎ 212/675-2626

550 Eighth Avenue
☎ 212/768-2255

Midtown Pool
371 West 34th Street
☎ 212/564-1071

If pool is not your game, how about bowling?
Ball Park Lanes is open until 3 A.M. Monday through Saturday
810 River Avenue, Bronx (across from Yankee Stadium),
☎ 718/665-5800.

Bowlmor Lanes is open until 4 A.M. Monday, Friday, and Saturday; until 2 on Thursday, and until 11 P.M. Tuesday and Wednesday.
110 University Place
(12th–13th Streets)
☎ 212/514-3705

Nighthawk iron pumpers can work out at three all-night gyms, although they probably have to become members first.

World Gym
1926 Broadway
☎ 212/874-0942

Crunch
404 Lafayette Street
☎ 212/614-0120

Johnny Lats
7 East 17th Street
☎ 212/366-4426

A two-hour tour of the **Fulton Fish Market** starts at 6 A.M. every Thursday, April through October. A guide tell you the history of this fascinating place, which dates from 1821, and takes you through the market, where you'll see many

The Fulton Fish Market

varieties of fish and shellfish being prepared for sale. Reservations are required. Fee: $10. Wear rubber-soled shoes. The tour leaves from the South Street Seaport Museum, 12 Fulton Street.
☎ 212/748-8590.

Jaywalking in Central Park doesn't involve dodging taxis; it's the name of the **Dawn Fitness Walk,** offered through the auspices of the NY Sports Club. It's a body-mind workout in a little-known part of the park, led by Jay Ciniglio, who

thought it up and named it after himself. The fee is $15 per class; 10 for $100. Participants meet Monday, Wednesday, and Saturday at the Fifth Avenue and East 85th Street entrance to the park.
☎ 212/860-8630

All Night Walking Tours are seasonal, offbeat tours, conducted by the 92nd Street Y. Phone for information.
☎ 212/996-1100

Steam Heat:
The Old-Fashioned Bath

Nothing is quite as refreshing as a steam bath followed by a cold shower. You can still enjoy this ancient custom at the **Tenth Street Turkish and Russian Baths.** Choose either Turkish-style (100 percent humidity) or the more popular Russian (50 percent humidity). When you've sweated to your content, screw up your courage and take an ice-cold Swedish shower or go into a frigid pool. Extend your pleasure with a massage, a Dead Sea body scrub, or a rubdown with an oak-leaf broom called a platza. A tiny restaurant offers fresh juices, salads, pickled herring, borscht, and stuffed cabbage. Hours: 9 A.M. to 10 P.M. daily (men only on Thursday and Sunday). Admission: $20; massage and treatments extra.
268 East 10th Street
(First Avenue–Avenue A)
☎ 212/473-8806

We've Got the Horse Right Here:
Riding in the City

There are several places in and around the city where you can rent a horse and ride to your heart's content. If you're an experienced English rider and want to ride in Central Park, there is only one choice, however: the **Claremont Riding Academy.** Built in 1892, it is the oldest continuously operated stable in the country. The emphasis is on instruction (private lessons are $40 a half hour), and there are six miles of bridle paths in the park to enjoy.
175 West 89th Street
(Amsterdam–Columbus Avenues)
☎ 212/724-5100

Claremont also has a facility in New Jersey called the **Overpeck Riding Center,** ☎ 201/944-7111.

A carriage ride in Central Park

Also in the city is the **Riverdale Equestrian Center.** It's open from 8 A.M. to 8 P.M. Tuesdays through Fridays, 8 A.M. to 5 P.M. Saturdays and Sundays. Riding and lessons are $60 an hour. The indoor ring permits year-long riding.
Broadway and 254th Street, Bronx
☎ 718/548-4848

There are three other convenient riding facilities:

Pelham Bay Stable
Pelham Bay Park, Shore Road, Bronx
☎ 718/885-0551
Private lessons: $35 a half hour,

$50 an hour (ages 8 and up). Trail rides: $35 a half hour, $50 and hour (ages 10 and up).

Jamaica Bay Riding Academy
7000 Shore Parkway (Broadway Ridge–70th Street), Brooklyn
☎ 718/531-8949
Trail rides: $20 for 45 minutes; lessons: $50 an hour, adults $30 a half hour, children $25.

Lynne's Riding Academy
88-03 70th Road (Sybilla Street–Metropolitan Avenue), Forest Hills
☎ 718/261-7679
Lessons are $25 a half hour, $50 an hour. Groups of three or more can

ride on the wooded trails in Forest Park for $20 an hour.

For fashion-conscious riders, **Miller's Harness Co.** carries proper riding clothing and fine English saddles.
117 East 24th Street
(Park–Lexington Avenues)
☎ 212/573-1400

Winston-Taylor's makes custom riding clothing, using traditional English fabrics.
11 East 44th Street
(Fifth–Madison Avenues)
☎ 212/687-0850

Double Axels and Places to Practice Them

The Wollman Rink in Central Park isn't the only place in the city to glide across the ice. The city can accommodate your needs, outdoors or indoors.

Other rinks include the one on the second level of the **World Trade Center.** Admission: adults $7, children $3.50. Skate rental: $3.50.
Church Street (Liberty–Vesey Streets)
☎ 212/435-4100

Ice Studio
1034 Lexington Avenue
(73rd–74th Streets)
☎ 212/535-0304
Admission for one hour: $5; ninety minutes: $6; skate rental: $2.75. Private lessons: $35 for a half hour. Phone first.

Lasker Rink
110th Street at Lenox Avenue
☎ 212/289-0599
Admission: $3.50 adults, $1.75 children. Skate rental: $3.25. Hours: 10 A.M. to 3 P.M. Mondays through Wednesdays, 10 A.M. to 10 P.M. Thursdays through Sundays.

Rivergate Ice Rink
401 East 34th Street (First Avenue)
☎ 212/684-5093
Outdoor rink. Hours: noon to 10 P.M. Mondays through Fridays. Admission: $6.50 adults, $3.50 children. Skate rental: $3.25.

Keep in Step, Keep in Shape

If you want to take long, brisk walks but your body doesn't, get in touch with The Walking Center of NYC, which conducts 90-minute classes in Central Park on weekends. A session combines work on body alignment with a cardiovascular walk. Fee: $10 a class. 212/580-1314

Rockefeller Center
Fifth and Sixth Avenues, West 49th and West 50th Streets
☎ 212/332-7654
Lower plaza. Open October to April. Four-hour periods begin at 9 A.M. (8:30 on weekends), with 30-minute breaks to clean the ice. Admission for adults: $7 weekdays, $8.50 weekends. Children: $6.50. Skate rental: $3.50.

Sky Rink
Chelsea Pier, 23rd Street and the Hudson River
☎ 212/336-6100
Two indoor rinks, one for skating, the other for hockey. Admission: $9 adults, $6.50 children. Skate rental: $3.50.

Shall We Dance? And Where?

New Yorkers have always enjoyed dancing, whatever their place on the social ladder. Dance halls for the working class were introduced to New York in the mid-1800s and soon developed a bad reputation. A certain John Allen, known as the "wickedest man in New York," ran a dance hall on Water Street that also was a bordello. Neighbors referred to Henry Hill's famous dance hall on Houston Street as the city's "most respectable disreputable house."

Dancing was also popular with the upper classes. Allan Dodsworth, a member of the New York Philharmonic, opened a dancing school on Broadway in 1843 that was well patronized by the social elite. Ragtime delighted the working classes and by 1895 there were some 130 dance halls in the city, most of them on the Lower East Side.

In the early twentieth century, two kinds of dance halls were popular. Dance palaces, like the Grand Central Palace on Lexington Avenue and the Savoy Ballroom catered to the young. The much smaller "taxi" dance halls offered female dance partners at a fixed price. During the Jazz Age in the 1920s, there were 786 licensed dance spaces in the five boroughs. The 1930s were the heyday of society orchestras playing in the ballrooms of the top city hotels.

The 1970s saw the coming of the discotheque. The city had more than its share: Cheetah on Broadway and 53rd Street, The Electric Circus at St. Mark's Place, Le Club in the Gotham Hotel, and, of course, the biggest of them all, Studio 54 on West 54th Street. They're all gone now but people still dance. Whatever kind of dance you prefer, it's waiting for you somewhere in the city.

Cafe Pierre, Pierre Hotel
2 East 61st Street (Fifth Avenue)
☎ 212/940-8185

Music from the '30s to the '50s is played by a trio for your dancing pleasure. Dress: jacket and tie for men, elegant for women. Cover charge: $10 if you don't have dinner in the hotel. Dancing from 9 P.M. to 1 A.M. Thursday through Saturday.

Les Poulets Cafe
16 West 22nd Street
(Fifth–Sixth Avenues)
☎ 212/229-2000

On one floor is a disco; the other has live Latin music on most weekends. The menu is Latin. Hours: 5 P.M. to varying after-midnight hours Wednesday through Sunday. No cover.

Marc Ballroom

27 Union Square
(West 16th–17th Streets)
☎ 212/867-3789

The deejay here plays both Latin and ballroom. Hours: 7 P.M. to midnight every other Sunday. Admission: $10.

New York Swing Dance Society

Irving Plaza at 17 Irving Place
(15th Street)
☎ 212/696-9737

You can dance to a live swing orchestra from 8 P.M. to midnight every Sunday. Admission: $13 for non-members. Phone for information about membership, practice nights, and lessons.

North River Bar

145 Hudson Street
(Hubert–Beach Streets)
☎ 212/226-9411

A deejay plays West Coast swing music for dancing here from 9 P.M. to midnight Tuesdays. Cover: $6.

Roseland Ballroom

239 West 52nd Street
(Eighth–Ninth Avenues)
☎ 212/247-0200

This landmark is as retro as they come. Ballroom dancing, Latin dancing in its many forms, disco, concerts—it all depends on what night you come. Phone for details. Hours: 2:30 P.M. to midnight Thursday and Sunday. Admission: $7 to $11. A cafeteria is available.

SOBs

204 Varick Street
(Seventh Avenue South)
☎ 212/243-4940

The acronym stands for Sounds of Brazil, and if the samba and other Brazilian dances are your forte, you've come to the right place. The cover charge varies, and dress is casual. Food: Brazilian/Caribbean. Call for schedule and hours.

Tatou

151 East 50th Street
(Lexington–Third Avenues)
☎ 212/753-1144

In this East Side American/French restaurant, a deejay spins "fast pop" after 11 every night but Sunday. Dinner is served from 5:30 P.M. to 11:30 P.M. A jacket and tie are required. Cover: $10–$20.

Several places described elsewhere in these pages also feature dancing. **The Rainbow Room** features a house orchestra that plays swing and alternates with a Latin band. **Red Blazer Too** has a 17-piece orchestra from 8 P.M. to midnight Tuesday. A live '40s swing band plays for dancing at the **Supper Club** on Friday and Saturday. At **Tavern on the Green,** patrons dance to a deejay's recorded music from 9 P.M. to closing Tuesday through Sunday. They dance outside during the summer. Patrons dance to recorded music before 9 P.M. at **View at the Marriott Marquis**. After 9 on Sunday and Monday, a jazz and top-40 group performs.

Studios That Teach the Latest Steps

In 1964 there were more than 20 Arthur Murray dance studios in New York, at least as many other licensed studios. "Killer Joe" Piro taught the mambo and the samba at the Palladium, at Broadway and 53rd Street. The dance scene is quieter now but if you're serious about dancing, the city has a number of studios where you can learn your choice of dance styles.

Dance Manhattan
39 West 15th Street (Fifth Avenue)
☎ 212/807-0802

Although dances are held several times a month, the accent is on lessons in ballroom and Latin dancing. Classes most nights at 8. Fee: $4 to $10.

Stepping Out
1780 Broadway (57th Street)
☎ 212/245-5200

Group classes for dancers of all levels cost $70 for a monthly series of four hour-long lessons.

DanceSport
1845 Broadway (60th Street)
☎ 212/307-1111

Group lessons in ballroom or Latin last 55 minutes and run in four-week cycles. Fee: $22 per class or four for $80. Private lessons cost $65 to $79 an hour.

Sandra Cameron Dance Center
20 Cooper Square (East 5th Street)
☎ 212/674-0505

Group lessons meet once a week and cost $65. The center also sponsors a series of Saturday evening dances at the 92nd Street Y.

Most dance companies have their own schools. Amateurs are welcome at these classes for beginners, which cost $10 and up.

Alvin Ailey American Dance Center
211 West 61st Street
(Amsterdam–West End Avenues)
☎ 212/767-0940

Ballet, tap, and modern dance.

American Ballet Theatre
890 Broadway (19th Street)
☎ 212/477-3030

Classical ballet.

The Well-Clad Dancer

Dancers need dancing shoes, tutus, and other items too numerous to mention. Capezio Dance-Theater Shop carries professional-quality shoes, plus practice and performance gear. 136 East 61st Street (Lexington–Park Avenues) 212/758-8833 and 1776 Broadway (57th Street) 212/586-5140.

Ballet Hispanico School of Dance
167 West 89th Street
(Columbus–Amsterdam Avenues)
☎ 212/362-6710
All styles of Latin and Spanish dance, including Flamenco.

Merce Cunningham Studio
55 Bethune Street
(Washington Avenue)
☎ 212/691-9751
Merce Cunningham technique.

Dance Space Inc.
662 Broadway
(Houston–Bleecker Streets)
☎ 212/777-8067
Simonson jazz, yoga, modern dance, ballet, and stretch.

Martha Graham School
316 East 63rd Street
(First–Second Avenues)
☎ 212/838-5886
Graham technique.

Lincoln Institute
611 Broadway
(Lafayette–Bleecker Streets)
☎ 212/777-3353
Jose Limon and Doris Humphrey technique.

Paul Taylor School
552 Broadway
(Prince–Spring Streets)
☎ 212/431-5562
Modern technique. Daily classes.

INTELLECTUAL PURSUITS

Checkmates: Where to Play the Game of Kings

The first national chess tournament was the First American Chess Congress, held in New York in 1817. It was won by Paul Morphy, a 20-year-old prodigy from New Orleans, who went on to become the best player in the world. For the next century New York was the center of American chess, attracting the best players, including the next three world champions, Wilhelm Steinitz, Emmanuel Lasker, and Jose Capablanca. In recent times, New York was the home of the remarkable world champion Bobby Fischer. The popularity of chess in New York can be seen in Greenwich Village's Washington Square Park on a summer's afternoon. Dozens of games will be in progress, many of them for high stakes.

The Village Chess Shop
230 Thompson Street
(West 3rd–Bleecker Streets)
☎ 212/475-9580

From noon to midnight, you can play chess in a club-like atmosphere on the tables here for a small hourly rate. It's also the place to purchase chess sets, plain or exotic, and chess boards in wood, glass, ceramic, or alabaster.

Chess Forum, on the same Greenwich Village block, has similar hours, policies, and wares.
219 Thompson Street
(West 3rd–Bleecker Streets)
☎ 212/475-2369

Ten Exciting Contemporary Art Galleries

No city in the world has more great art museums than New York, and you can spend your free time enjoying their collections. But you should also visit contemporary galleries to see what's happening in the art world today. Some works will shock you, some will baffle you, and some will delight you. Seeing new things with an open mind is critical to developing an eye for art. Here are some of cutting-edge galleries, uptown and downtown:

Michael Werner
21 East 67th Street
(Madison–Fifth Avenues)
☎ 212/988-1623

Rising European stars, including Marcel Broodthaers, Sigmar Polke, and Per Kirkeby.

Mary Boone
745 Fifth Avenue
(57th–58th Streets)
☎ 212/752-2929

The place to see the works of Ross Bleckner, Eric Fischl, and Barbara Kruger.

Andre Emmerich
41 East 57th Street
(Madison–Fifth Avenues)
☎ 212/752-0120

Pieces by Anthony Caro, Dorothea Rockburne, Judy Pfaff, and David Hockney.

Alexander and Bonin
132 Tenth Avenue
(18th–19th Streets)
☎ 212/367-7474

Painting, sculpture, photography and works on paper by young international artists, including Doris Saledo, Willie Doherty, Ree Morton, and Paul Thek.

303 Gallery
525 West 22nd Street
(Tenth–Eleventh Avenues)
☎ 212/255-1121

Internationalist artists, including photographers Thomas Ruff and Collier Schorr, sculptor Daniel Oates, and painters Sue Williams and Karen Kilimnik.

Urban Birdwatching

NYC Audubon Society
700 Broadway (East 4th Street)
212/979-3000

The society conducts birdwatching outings in Central Park, Jamaica Bay, and other locations nearby. Volunteers are welcome to participate in the spring and winter bird counts, called Birdathons. Fee: $4 for members.

The Urban Park Rangers lead birdwatching tours in city parks. Call 360-2774 or 800-NY-PARKS. You can hear daily announcements of bird sittings by phoning Rare Bird Alert, 212/979-3070.

Paul Kasmin
74 Grand Street
(Wooster–Greene Streets)
☎ 212/219-3219

Rising stars, including Donald Bachler, Alessandro Twombly, Suzanne McClelland, and Elliot Puckette.

Postmasters
80 Greene Street
(Prince–Grand Streets)
☎ 212/941-5711

An important international gallery; conceptual art in a wide variety of media.

David Zwirner
43 Greene Street
(Broome–Grand Streets)
☎ 212/966-9074

Artists include Raymond Pettibon,

Toba Khedoori, Stan Douglas, and Jason Rhodes.

Holly Solomon Gallery
172 Mercer Street (Houston Street)
☎ 212/941-5777

Distinctive work in all media from such artists as Nam June Paik, Izhar Patkin, and Nick Walpington.

Gagosian
136 Wooster Street
(Houston–Prince Streets)
☎ 212/228-2828

A big space for big works. Artists include Ellen Gallagher and Britain's Jake and Dinos Chapman.

Freebies on the Cultural Front

These New York museums and institutions offer free admission at these times:

Asia Society, 6–8 P.M. Tuesday
Bronx Museum of the Arts, 3–9 P.M. Wednesday
Bronx Zoo, 10 A.M.–5:30 P.M. Wednesday
Cooper-Hewitt National Design Museum, 5–9 P.M. Tuesday
Solomon R. Guggenheim Museum, 6–8 P.M. Friday

International Center of Photography, 5–8 P.M. Friday
Jewish Museum, 5–8 P.M. Tuesday
Museum of Modern Art, 4:30–5:15 P.M. Friday
New Museum of Contemporary Art, 6–8 P.M. Thursday
New York Botanical Garden, 10 A.M.–noon Wednesday, 10 A.M.–noon Saturday
Whitney Museum of American Art, 6–8 P.M. first Thursday of every month

Inside the Guggenheim

Ten Classic New York Movies

More movies have been set in New York than in any other American city. In fact, New York was a center of film production years before the sunny skies of California lured producers west in the early 1900s. D. W. Griffith liked to film here, and many of Mack Sennett's *Keystone Cops* comedies were filmed in Coney Island. Here are some of the best films to feature New York:

All About Eve (1950) "Fasten your seat belts; it's going to be a bumpy night!" An ambitious and ruthless young actress (Anne Baxter) tangles with an aging Broadway star (Bette Davis). George Sanders is superb as an acerbic drama critic. The film won five Academy Awards, including best picture, supporting actor, and two to Joseph Mankiewicz for both writer and director.

Breakfast at Tiffany's (1961) The movie version of Truman Capote's story of a charmingly goofy call girl with an exotic social and emotional life isn't great, but Audrey Hepburn as Holly Golightly is. The great supporting cast includes George Peppard, Patricia Neal, and Mickey Rooney. Also great: Henry Mancini's Academy Award–winning "Moon River."

The Godfather (1972) The head of a New York mafia family (Marlon Brando) dies of old age and his son (Al Pacino) takes over. The film won Academy Awards for best picture and best actor (Brando). Part II is almost as good.

The French Connection (1971) New York police, led by detective Popeye Doyle (Gene Hackman), track down a consignment of drugs entering the country in a car. The movie was based on the exploits of NYPD detective Eddie Egan, a tough, rule-breaking cop. Memorable scenes include a car chase under the elevated railway in Queens, and Hackman standing in the rain, looking through a window at the villain (Fernando Rey) lunching in a fashionable East Side restaurant.

Laura (1944) A beautiful woman is murdered—we think. This ageless adult mystery has a brilliantly spare script and a marvelous cast. Gene Tierney is Laura, Dana Andrews is the smitten detective, and Clifton Webb is marvelous as Waldo Lydecker.

Manhattan (1979) The movie chronicles the complex love life of a TV comedy writer, played by Woody Allen, who is obsessed—as he is in real life—with New York. The film is notable for its outstanding performances by Allen, Diane Keaton, Meryl Streep, Mariel Hemingway, and the New York Philharmonic, which plays the background music. Many think this was Woody Allen's masterpiece.

Miracle on 34th Street (1947) A department store Santa Claus (Edmund Gwenn) claims to be the real thing. John Payne and Maureen O'Hara are the lovers; Natalie Wood, the little girl.

Moonstruck (1987) A young widow (Cher) falls for the estranged brother (Nicolas Cage) of her husband-to-be (Danny Aiello). Cher won the Academy Award for best actress. Olympia Dukakis also was superb.

Saturday Night Fever (1977) A young Brooklyn shoe salesman (John Travolta) lives for disco dancing until he falls for his dancing partner (Karen Lynn Gorney), who teaches him that there are other things in life. The dance numbers are great, and the movie launched Travolta's film career.

Yankee Doodle Dandy (1942) Jimmy Cagney, who grew up on the Upper East Side and was a Broadway hoofer before going to Hollywood, won the Academy Award for his portrayal of Mr. Broadway himself, George M. Cohan. This is a star turn if there ever was one.

Parlez Vous . . . ?
Learning a New Language

More languages are spoken in New York than even the most gifted linguist could learn in a lifetime. But being able to communicate in more than one language is helpful and fun. You may wish to learn another language or brush up on one you vaguely remember from your school days. A second language can open many new doors to you, here and abroad.

If you prefer classroom instruction, **New York University** teaches 25 languages in many kinds of programs.
50 West 4th Street
(Mercer Street–La Guardia Place)
☎ 212/998-7080

The New School teaches 16 languages, including sign language.
66 West 12th Street
(Fifth–Sixth Avenues)
☎ 212/229-5690

The World Trade Institute Language Center teaches ten.
1 World Trade Center
☎ 212/435-4074

Alliance Francaise offers French classes at every level.
22 East 60th Street
(Madison–Park Avenues)
☎ 212/355-6100

The China Institute teaches Mandarin and Cantonese.
125 East 65th Street
(Park–Lexington Avenues)
☎ 212/744-8181

Deutsches Haus at NYU teaches beginning and intermediate German and offers conversational classes. Day and evening schedules are available.
42 Washington Mews (Washington Square–La Guardia Place)
☎ 212/988-8660

Scuola Italiana, in Our Lady of Pompeii, offers two-month courses in Italian which were developed at the University of Perugia. All teachers are natives who have taught in Italy.
240 Bleecker Street
(Carmine–Leroy Streets)
☎ 212/229-1361

Japan Society offers the largest Japanese language program in the United States. Twelve levels are taught in classes that are limited to 20 students.
333 East 47th Street
(First–Second Avenues)
☎ 212/715-1256

Spanish Institute offers a full range of classes from beginner to "superior," and all stress the conversational "natural approach."
684 Park Avenue
(68th–69th Streets)
☎ 212/628-0420

Bibliophile Delights: Some Favorite Bookstores

The first bookstore in the city opened in 1693, and bookstores have been part of the city ever since. Colonial bookstores also served as post offices and often sold stationery and dry goods. By 1870 August Brentano, an Austrian immigrant, had opened Brentano's Literary Emporium on Union Square, and it was a meeting house for writers like Henry Ward Beecher, Edwin Booth, and Artemus Ward.

Today few if any cities can match New York for good bookstores. It's a comforting feeling to know that the book you seek is out there in the city somewhere. On-line book sellers are lifesavers if you live in Nevada or North Dakota, but there is no substitute for being able to hold a book in your hands and look through it before buying it. New York is a godsend to browsers. Here is a sampling of New York's finest bookstores:

Ten Great Non-Fiction Books about New York

A History of New York, from the Beginning of the World to the End of the Dutch Dynasty, Diedrich Knickerbocker
Notes of a Native Son, James Baldwin
Here Is New York, E. B. White
The Kingdom and the Glory, Gay Talese
Up in the Old Hotel, Joseph Mitchell
Broadway, Brooks Atkinson
Deadline: A Memoir, James Reston
The Big Money, John Dos Passos
'Tis, Frank McCourt
Damon Runyon, Jimmy Breslin

Academy

10 West 18th Street
(Fifth–Sixth Avenues)
☎ 212/242-4848

This is a well-stocked secondhand bookstore on the northern edge of Greenwich Village. The staff is particularly helpful.

Skyline, across the street from Academy, is also a small, good bookstore.
13 West 18th Street
(Fifth–Sixth Avenues)
☎ 212/759-5463

Coliseum Coliseum is a big, well-stocked, no-frills, no-nonsense store. Downstairs are deals on hard covers. The store is open late.
1771 Broadway (57th Street)
☎ 212/757-8381

Gotham

41 West 47th Street
(Fifth–Sixth Avenues)
☎ 212/719-4448

This midtown bookstore has made a lot of friends since it opened in 1920, and it has all the history and atmosphere you might expect. In the art book department upstairs is a small gallery where occasional exhibitions are presented.

Rizzoli

31 West 57th Street
(Fifth–Sixth Avenues)
☎ 212/759-2424

This is the most beautiful bookstore in the city. The store is particularly well stocked with art books.

The Strand

828 Broadway (East 12th Street)
☎ 212/473-1452

A branch of the Strand is at 95 Fulton Street (Front Street)
☎ 212/732-6070.

This bookstore advertises "miles and miles of books," and it doesn't exaggerate. Its huge collection includes thousands of review copies of new books, coffee-table books, and tables loaded with mass-market and trade paperbacks, all sold at discount. It's a literary landmark, open daily.

SPECIALTY BOOKSTORES

ARCHITECTURE

Urban Center Books
457 Madison Avenue
(50th–51st Streets)
☎ 212/935-3595

ART

Hacker Art Books
45 West 57th Street
(Fifth–Sixth Avenues)
☎ 212/688-7600

Ursus Books
Mezzanine of the Carlyle Hotel,
981 Madison Avenue
(76th–77th Streets)
☎ 212/772-8787
Ursus is also on the third floor at
375 West Broadway
(Spring–Broome Streets)
☎ 212/226-7858

FASHION

Fashion Design Books
234 West 27th Street
(Seventh–Eighth Avenues)
☎ 212/633-9646

HISTORY

Argosy
116 East 59th Street
(Park–Lexington Avenues)
☎ 212/753-4455

Ideal Book Store
547 West 110th Street
(Amsterdam Avenue)
☎ 212/662-1909

Ten Great Novels about New York

The Alienist, **Caleb Carr**
archy and mehitabel, **Don Marquis**
Bonfire of the Vanities, **Tom Wolfe**
Breakfast at Tiffany's, **Truman Capote**
Butterfield 8, **John O'Hara**
Time and Again, **Jack Finney**
Invisible Man, **Ralph Ellison**
Last Exit to Brooklyn, **Hubert Selby Jr.**
Ragtime, **E. L. Doctorow**
Washington Square, **Henry James**

MILITARY

The Military Bookman
29 East 93rd Street
(Fifth–Madison Avenues)
☎ 212/348-1280

MYSTERIES

The Black Orchid
303 East 81st Street
(Fifth–Madison Avenues)
☎ 212/734-5980

Murder Ink
2486 Broadway
(92nd–93rd Streets)
☎ 212/362-8905
Also at 1465 Second Avenue
(76th–77th Streets)
☎ 212/517-3222

The Mysterious Bookshop
129 West 56th Street
(Sixth–Seventh Avenues)
☎ 212/765-0900

Partners & Crime
44 Greenwich Avenue
(6th–7th Streets)
☎ 212/243-0440

PHOTOGRAPHY
A Photographer's Place
133 Mercer Street
(Prince–Spring Streets)
☎ 212/431-9358

THEATER, FILM, TV
Applause
211 West 71st Street
(Broadway–West End Avenue)
☎ 212/496-7511

Drama Bookshop
723 Seventh Avenue
(48th–49th Streets)
☎ 944-0595

Richard Stoddard Performing Arts Books
18 East 16th Street
(Fifth–Union Square West)
☎ 212/645-9576

TRAVEL
Complete Traveller
199 Madison Avenue (35th Street)
☎ 212/685-9007

OUT AND ABOUT

Going, Going, Gone!
The Auction Scene

There were auctions in the city from the earliest days of colonial rule. In fact, the first auction laws were enacted in 1676. Auctions are fun, particularly if you buy the right thing at the right price. Auctions are also a good way to learn more about art, or whatever is being auctioned. If you're not careful, however, you'll get caught up in the bidding frenzy and spend more than you'd planned, or buy something you didn't want.

To avoid the perils of an auction, we suggest that you attend the auction preview and purchase the catalog. See what's going to be auctioned off, decide what you want, then set your top price and stick to it.

A good place to learn about auctions is **William Doyle,** which holds several auctions every month, with special ones for Lalique, majolica, Belle Epoque, and couture, each only once a year. The Tag Sale, held next door to the main auction house, has "treasure auctions" of more affordable items. Doyle offers auction neophytes lectures on aspects of collecting and restoration. On Tuesday morning you can have an item appraised free of charge.
175 East 87th Street
(Lexington–Third Avenues)
☎ 212/427-4885

Christie's is one of the two top auction houses in the city, regularly handling art sales in the multimillion-dollar class. The high seasons are May and November. Check the Friday and Sunday art pages in the *Times* for upcoming sales.
502 Park Avenue (59th Street)
☎ 212/636-2000

Christie's East auctions less expensive merchandise. Its high seasons are June and December.
219 East 67th Street
(Second–Third Avenues)
☎ 212/606-0400

Sotheby's
1334 York Avenue (72nd Street)
☎ 212/606-7000

This is the other top auction house.

It holds more than 500 sales annually, which peak during May and November. A ticket is necessary for evening sales. Be prepared to pay for your successful bid on the spot. Sotheby's Education Department (212/750-6318) offers lectures and one- to three-day seminars on such topics as American furniture or setting a holiday table with antique dishes. There is also a nine-month accredited course on American Arts, many graduates of which go on to work in the antique or auction fields.

A lot of things other than art are auctioned in New York. **Leland Auction House** holds two auctions of sports memorabilia a year. Recent sales at Leland's included Jackie Robinson's hat and Babe Ruth's uniform. The auction atmosphere is festive. The auctions, held at the Southgate Towers Hotel near Madison Square Garden, last two days.
☎ 212/545-0800

Morrell & Co.
535 Madison Avenue
(54th–55th Streets)

In 1994, Morrell held the first live public auction of wines since Prohibition. Now it has four wine auctions a year at the Union League, 37th and Park. The accent is on the old and the rare. Phone
☎ **212/688-9370** for a pamphlet that explains the bidding procedures.

Swann Galleries
104 East 25th Street
(Park–Lexington Avenues)
☎ 212/254-4710

Some 35 times a year, Swann auctions rare American books, maps, atlases, autographs, manuscripts, photographs, and works of art on paper. Auctions are held Thursday evenings, and works to be auctioned are on view the preceding Saturday and Monday through Wednesday. Map auctions generally occur in May and December.

Lend a Hand:
Volunteer Opportunities

To be happy, make someone else happy. You can test the validity of this bit of folk wisdom by volunteering some of your time to one of these worthy causes:

AIDS Care Center of New York Hospital–Cornell Medical Center,
525 East 68th Street
☎ 212/746-5454

Evelyn H. Lauder Breast Center of Memorial Sloan-Kettering Cancer Center
205 East 64th Street
☎ 212/639-5200

Hale House
300 Manhattan Avenue
☎ 212/663-0700

Harvard AIDS Institute, c/o Harvard Club of New York City
27 West 44th Street
☎ 212/840-6600

Henry Street Settlement
265 Henry Street
☎ 212/766-9200

Ronald McDonald House
405 East 73rd Street
☎ 212/639-0100

Salvation Army
120 West 14th Street
☎ 212/337-6200

United Way
99 Park Avenue
☎ 212/973-3800

 # Time on Your Hands: Finding Vintage Watches

A vintage wristwatch is an ever-present reminder of good times past, and if you shop wisely it can be a good investment as well. A variation on this theme is the character watch. The Mickey Mouse watch, which debuted in 1933, was the first and most successful character watch; it saved the Ingersoll Co. from bankruptcy. Macy's once sold 11,000 Mickeys in a single day. There also were Betty Boop watches, Dick Tracy watches, product watches promoting Ritz Crackers, Spam, Tabasco and Tom Mix for Ralston Purina. Sports watches commemorated such heroes as Mickey Mantle and Muhammad Ali, and political watches featured presidential candidates.

Aaron Faber
666 Fifth Avenue (53rd Street)
☎ 212/586-8411

Wristwatches were first worn during World War I, and for some years men who wore them were considered sissies. Mr. Faber offers "high-grade European and American rarities" from 1950 to 1960, the peak collectible period. His shop also services and restores vintage watches. All vintage watches are guaranteed for one year.

Time Will Tell
962-A Madison Avenue
(75th–76th Streets)
☎ 212/861-2663

Proprietor Stewart Unger offers watches from a $65 quartz with a pig on the dial to top-quality vintage watches which command five-figure prices. All are in working order and guaranteed for a year and a day. Mr. Unger is the co-author, with Edward Faber, of *American Wristwatches—Five Decades of Style and Design*. The shop will test mechanical watches for accuracy on a Vibrograph, a machine that measures the ticking mechanism and gives a paper readout.

Christie's has watch and clock auctions several times a year. Vivian Swift, Christie's watch historian, is available for private appraisals.
20 Rockefeller Plaza
☎ 212/636-2000

Cartier has a search service for people looking for vintage Cartier watches. Phone Ellen Devera at ☎ 212/446-3483.

Maggie Kenyon
By appointment only, 212/675-3213. Maggie Kenyon specializes in character watches in perfect condition, the prices of which can range from $200 to the thousands.

Tourneau
58th Street and Madison Avenue
☎ 212/758-6234

Probably the largest selection of watches new and old is at this well-known store. You can buy, sell, or trade. Estimates and repairs are also available.

Central Watchband Stand, Ltd.
☎ 212/685-1689

This stand in Grand Central Station has a wide selection of vintage watches, which it also repairs.

Flea Markets

There are treasures galore to be found at flea markets, and half the fun is poking around the stands. The action is on Sixth Avenue in Chelsea.

Annex Antiques Fair and Flea Market
110 West 19th Street (Annex)
West 24th–27th Streets (Fair)
☎ 212/243-5343

The Annex is open Sunday. The Antiques Fair, open Saturday and Sunday, charges $1 admission. Both are outdoors and open from 9 A.M. to 5 P.M., weather permitting. The Grand Bazaar, where more than 100 dealers exhibit, also is held here.

Metropolitan Book Center has a number of rare-book dealers and holds special book events; phone for a schedule.
123 West 18th Street
(Sixth–Seventh Avenues)
☎ 212/929-4488

Metropolitan Antiques Building
110 West 19th Street
(Sixth–Seventh Avenues)
☎ 212/463-0200

Special shows and auctions are held at this site, which is closed in July and August. Phone for a schedule of events.

Chelsea Antiques Building
110 West 25th Street
(Sixth–Seventh Avenues)
☎ 212/929-0909

The 12 floors here house 75 dealers.

Lucille's Antique Emporium
126 West 26th Street
(Sixth–Seventh Avenues)
☎ 212/691-1041

The specialty here is linens from the '40s and '50, and you'll find damask bedcovers, linen sheets, and printed tablecloths. Also on display are vintage designer clothing, costume jewelry, and millinery. Hours: noon to 7:30 P.M. Tuesday through Friday.

Columbus Avenue Flea Market
(76th–77th Streets)
Hours: 9 A.M. to 5 P.M. Sunday.

SoHo/Canal Street Flea Market
Corner of Broadway and Grand
Hours: 9 A.M. to 5 P.M. Saturday and Sunday.

The Pleasures of Street Fairs

New York has always had a vibrant street life. In colonial times business was often conducted outdoors. Stocks were traded near a buttonwood tree between 68 and 70 Wall Street. Prior to 1841 meats and vegetables had to be sold in public markets rather than private shops. Other kinds of street vendors also were common in the early days. Among the products sold were gingerbread, roasted peanuts, apple cider, kindling, shoelaces, brooms, and newspapers. Children incorporated into their games stoops, cornices, manhole covers, curbs, and fire escapes. In addition, street celebrations have always been an important part of neighborhood identity. Little wonder that New Yorkers love a street fair; it's in their blood. A street fair offers good things to eat, games to play, interesting people to mingle with, lots of things to see and do. On weekends from early spring to late fall, there's usually a street fair somewhere in the city. Here's a sampling of some of the old favorites. Check a local newspaper or call the New York City Visitors' Bureau for dates and times of these fairs:

Ninth Avenue International Festival
(37th–57th Streets)
Food booths line the avenue. Mid-May.

Midtown Chinese Spring Festival
31st Street
(Lexington–Park Avenues)
You can see colorful costumes and sample food from the various regions of China. Mid-May.

Greek Orthodox Church of St. Demetrios Festival
152nd Street (84th Road–84th Drive) Jamaica, Queens
Lovers of souvlaki and other Greek delicacies flock here every spring. Last weekend in May.

Our Lady of Lebanon Cathedral
Remsen Street (Clinton–Henry Streets) Brooklyn Heights
Festival Lebanese food is the attraction here. Last weekend in May.

A street fair on Third Avenue

Brooklyn Arts and Culture Parks Jamboree
718/783-4469

This festival takes place at several locations in June. Phone for details.

Asian-American Festival Day
Columbus Park, Bayard and Mulberry Streets, Chinatown

You can sample exotic food and see the dances of Japan, Thailand, Vietnam, and Korea. Last weekend in June.

Ebenezer Wesleyan Methodist Church Fair
Bergen Street (Nostrand–Rogers Avenues), Bedford-Stuyvesant, Brooklyn

This festival features Caribbean food and Caribbean music. Late June.

International African Arts Festival
Fulton Street (Utica–Schenectady Avenues) Bedford-Stuyvesant, Brooklyn

Music, arts and crafts, and food from Africa, the Caribbean, and the American South are featured. First weekend in July.

Bastille Day
60th Street (Park–Fifth Avenues)

This festival features New Orleans Jazz, plus French food and wine from local cafes. On or around July 14.

Taste of Times Square
West 46th Street (Broadway–Ninth Avenues)

You can sample food from the restaurants of Restaurant Row. Mid-July.

Fiesta De Santiago
West 14th Street

Little Spain celebrates with food, crafts, and mariachi music. Last weekend of July.

Harlem Week
West 125th Street
(Lenox–Seventh Avenues)

This celebration actually lasts for 2½ weeks in late August. On the final weekend, jazz bands and dancers create "Uptown Saturday Night."

Richmond County Fair
715 Ocean Terrace, Staten Island

Staten Island celebrates with pig races, armadillo derbies, antique cars, pie-eating contests, and other fair attractions. September.

Atlantic Antic
Atlantic Avenue in Cobble Hill, Brooklyn

Brooklyn turns out for the fun in September.

Amsterdam Avenue Festival
(77th–92nd Streets)

During the summer a festival is held on every third Sunday of the month.

Eighth Avenue Festival
(42nd–57th Streets)
Food booths line the avenue in early November.

Little Touches of Green: A Guide to Gardens and Pocket Parks

Manhattan isn't all steel and concrete. When you least expect it, you'll come across little touches of green, some of which offer other inducements.

Bryant Park
Sixth Avenue
(West 40th–West 42nd Streets)

Behind the main branch of the Public Library is a serene and formal garden with quite a history. Once a potter's field, it became the site of the four-acre Croton Reservoir, with walls 50 feet high and 25 feet thick. In 1853, after the reservoir was demolished, an imitation of London's Crystal Palace was build on the park, but it burned down in 1858. Troops used the park as a drill field during the Civil War.

McGraw-Hill Building
West 49th Street
(Sixth–Seventh Avenues)

Along the side is a small park built inside the plaza. Go down the stairs and you'll find a stone bench. Look inside and you'll see the Pool of Planets. The gold line in the center is the sun, and nine spheres show the relation of the planets to the sun.

Museum of Modern Art
11 West 53rd Street
(Fifth–Sixth Avenues)

One of the treasures of this marvelous museum is its garden, a perfect urban oasis. In it is sculpture by Rodin, Renoir, Miro, Matisse, Picasso, and other modern masters. Concerts are held in the garden each summer. One must visit the museum to visit the garden, which is open the same hours as the museum.

Paley Park
East 53rd Street
(Fifth–Madison Avenues)

Where Sherman Billingsley's Stork Club once stood is a small park, a gift from William Paley, founder and former chairman of CBS. It has a wall of flowing water, a refreshment stand, and usually a lovely breeze.

IBM Garden
56th Street and Madison Avenue

Although it's in the building, this is a great place to rest from the pressures of midtown. The setting includes lots of glass, high ceilings, trees, chairs and tables, and an excellent refreshment stand.

Greenacre Park
21 East 51st Street
(Fifth–Madison Avenues)

This is another midtown oasis, with soothing waterfalls, granite walls, tables, chairs, and a refreshment stand. The park was a gift to the city by the daughter of John D. Rockefeller.

Rockefeller Center
Bounded by West 48th and West 52nd, Fifth and Seventh Avenues

The touches of green here have been described elsewhere in these pages.

Ford Foundation Building
East 42nd Street
(First–Second Avenues)

One of the city's most handsome buildings wraps itself around trees, an indoor garden, and a pool. If you walk through, you'll see what inspired architecture can do for the soul.

Tudor City
East 40th to East 43rd Streets
(First–Second Avenues)

Across the street from the Ford Foundation Building is Tudor City, which was an ambitious private renewal project in the 1920s. It includes 12 buildings, with some 3,000 apartments, restaurants, shops, and its own post office. It is wrapped around its own open space and is well worth exploring.

The Museum of Modern Art

2 Dag Hammarskjold Plaza
Second Avenue

This office building is set on an elevated terrace, which displays outdoor sculpture.

United Nations
Entrance at East 45th Street and First Avenue

The UN tour doesn't include the gardens, which is a shame. The Peace Garden, for example, has more than a thousand rosebushes of hundreds of varieties. And a walk along the East River is a restful way to spend an hour at noon or late afternoon.

No-name park
This is one of our favorite havens, although we never found out its name, or even if it had a name. From the east end of East 51st Street, steps lead down to a small park and a footbridge over FDR Drive. Cross the bridge and you'll look back at Beekman Place and a view of the drive disappearing under a Sutton Place apartment house. Across the river you'll see Roosevelt Island. Chances are you'll have the place to yourself.

Sutton Square
59th Street and Sutton Place

This small park is pure New York romance. You have a view of the 59th Street Bridge, frolicking kids, and some of the great town houses in the city. If you have *déjà vu*, it may be because it has been used in a number of movies. Woody Allen and Diane Keaton had their first date here in *Manhattan*.

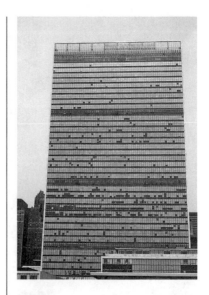

The United Nations Plaza

Damrosch Park
West 65th Street and Broadway

This park is part of Lincoln Center. During the day it offers trees and benches, but two evenings a week during the summer classical music is performed, sponsored by WQXR, the city's only classical music station, and Lincoln Center Out-of-Doors.

Madison Square
Bounded by East 23rd and East 26th Streets, Madison and Fifth Avenues

When the city created its grid street pattern in 1811, this former potter's field and parade ground became a park, and soon a fashionable residential district surrounded it. After the Civil War, the fancy Fifth

Avenue Hotel, the Madison Square Theater, and the second home of Madison Square Garden faced the square. Today it is ringed by office buildings, but it still retains an air of serenity.

Washington Square
Bounded by University Place and MacDougal Street, West 4th Street and Waverly Place

The city's gallows were located here until it became a public park and parade ground in the 1820s. The Memorial Arch, where Fifth Avenue ends at the park, was first erected in wood for the celebration of 1876, then Stanford White designed it in stone. Fashionable houses then were built around the park. Today Greenwich Village life centers around the square. You'll see performers, chess players, orators, and markets and fairs on the weekends.

Washington Market Park
Greenwich and Chambers Streets

This is a relatively new park, built for the community on the grounds of Manhattan Community College, and it's a beauty. It has a great view of the Hudson River. The residents of TriBeCa do a commendable job of caring for the grounds and garden.

Rector Park
Outside Liberty Court at Rector Place in Battery City

This park was built recently as an amenity for the residents of Battery City. It has attractive sculpture, flower beds, shrubbery, and a great view across the harbor of New Jersey and the Statue of Liberty.

Rockefeller Park
Located on the side of Battery City, next to the World Trade Center

Madison Square Garden

There is yet another new park in the Financial District. It offers the weary great harbor vistas, grass slopes to lie on, and free concerts on Tuesday nights in the summer.

Battery Park
Bounded by Whitehall Street, the Hudson, and Battery Place

This park at the foot of Manhattan Island takes its name from a line of British cannons that faced the harbor in the late 1600s. Now it's a buffer between the canyons of Wall Street and the harbor. In the park is a World War II memorial, a Korean War memorial, and the 100,000-rose Hope Garden, a living memorial to those who have died of AIDS.

Where to Stop to Smell the Flowers

For a city of steel and concrete, New York has a surprising number of large gardens. Some are near the city boundaries, but most are either in the heart of town or near the centers of each borough. All will help relieve the anxieties of the city. All are worth visiting.

Abby Aldrich Rockefeller Sculpture Garden, Museum of Modern Art
11 West 53rd Street
(Fifth–Sixth Avenues)
☎ 212/708-9460

This is a delightful combination of trees, shrubs, pools, fountains, and statuary. The garden includes weeping beeches, Lombardy poplars, hornbeams, andromeda, ivy, and seasonal plants. Ample benches and other seating are available. Open to 6 P.M. daily.

Bartow-Pell Mansion and Gardens
895 Shore Road North,
Pelham Bay Park, Queens
☎ 718/885-1461

This stately manor house has terraced gardens leading to a pool. The setting is particularly beautiful in the spring. Hours: noon to 4 P.M. Wednesday, Saturday, and Sunday. Admission: adults $2, students and seniors $1.25, children under 12 free.

Brooklyn Botanic Garden
1000 Washington Avenue (Empire Boulevard–Eastern Parkway)
☎ 718/622-7200

The highlights here include such celebrated plantings as a Japanese hill-and-pond garden, an herb garden with more than 300 specimens, and one of the largest public rose collections in America. The Steinhardt Conservatory houses the largest bonsai collection in the country. The 50 acres of flora include a fragrance garden for the blind. The master plan of the garden was designed by the Olmsted brothers and installed in 1910; the landscaping was completed two years later, and the Steinhardt Conservatory was added in 1988. Flowering is heaviest from mid-April through June. Hours: 8 A.M. to 6 P.M. Tuesday to Friday, 10 to 6 weekends and holidays. Steinhardt Conservatory is open the same hours Tuesday through Sunday. Admission: $3; free Tuesday.

Central Park
The park is completely landscaped with trees, shrubs, meadows, and lawns, and contains several ponds and a lake. There is a delightful conservatory garden on the site of the old greenhouse at 105th Street and Fifth Avenue, where seasonal displays are exhibited. Other informal plantings are distributed throughout the park. Note the magnolias and flowering crab apples in the spring. Also in the park are a Shakespeare Garden and a meandering walk called a Ramble. Hours: sunrise to sunset daily. For information, stop at the Central Park Dairy, mid-park at 65th Street.
☎ 212/794-6564

Rockefeller Center Channel Gardens
Fifth Avenue at 49th Street
☎ 212/247-4777

Rockefeller Center was the first large project to use landscaping at both street and rooftop levels. The Channel Gardens, an allée between several buildings, have six formal beds, plus fountains and benches; the rooftops, all told, have nearly two acres of gardens. More than 20,000 plants are displayed in the Channel Gardens—lilies in the spring, tropical plants in the summer, chrysanthemums in the fall, and a special illuminated display during the Christmas season. Among the mini-park gardens on the rooftops are raised tree beds, sculptures, a reflecting pool, fountains, lawns, and clipped hedges. The Channel Gardens are open at all times; the roof gardens only on special tours, for which a fee is charged.

United Nations Garden
First Avenue at East 45th Street
☎ 212/963-1234

This is a small island of peace in a noisy part of the city. The Peace Garden contains more than a thousand rosebushes. Open daily 9–5.

The Cloisters
Fort Tryon Park, Northern Avenue and Cabrini Circle
212/923-3700

The attraction here is medieval gardens faithfully and beautifully reproduced. Iris is featured in the Cuxa Cloister, Christmas plants in the Saint-Guilhem Cloister, 140 varieties of herbs in the Bonnefont Cloister, fragrant herbs in the courtyard—seventy of them from the list that Charlemagne compiled for his own chateau garden, and eighty more from old herbal lists. Hours: 9:30 A.M. to 5:15 P.M. Tuesdays through Sundays. Closed some holidays; phone ahead to check. Suggested contribution: $10 adults, $5 students and seniors.

Courtyard Gardens, Frick Collection
1 East 70th Street (Fifth Avenue)
☎ 212/288-0700

This is arguably the outstanding courtyard garden in the city. Built of limestone and several kinds of marble, it has a central fountain and flowering plants and shrubs, including gardenias, cinerarias, and exotic foliage plants, which are moved as required.

Dyckman House Park and Museum
4881 Broadway (West 204th Street)
☎ 212/304-9433

This garden of boxwood hedges, flowers, fruit trees, and a grape arbor is reminiscent, as is the house, of Dutch design. Hours: 11 A.M. to 4 P.M. Tuesdays through Sundays. Free admission.

Ford Foundation Indoor Garden
320 East 43rd Street
(First–Second Avenues)
☎ 212/573-5000

The eleven-story building encloses an indoor garden containing trees, flowers, shrubs, and vines that bloom most of the year. The garden is surrounded on two sides by L-shaped office wings, and on the other two sides by ten-story-high glass walls. Southern magnolias and jacaranda, azaleas and camellias, helxine and Korean grass are among the numerous collections of plants. Hours: 9 A.M. to 5 P.M. Monday through Friday. Free admission.

Biblical Garden at the Cathedral of St. John the Divine
1047 Amsterdam Avenue
(112th Street)
☎ 212/361-7540

On the grounds of the world's largest Gothic cathedral, this quarter-acre garden contains more than 1100 kinds of plants that are mentioned in the Bible, including flowers, herbs and bitter herbs (chicory, dandelion), grains, and vegetables. All plantings are labeled with pertinent biblical verses. Cedars, pines, walnuts, willows, and cypresses shade the benches along the paths. Hours: 7 A.M. to sunset daily. Admission free.

Fort Tryon Park
190th Street and Overlook Terrace
☎ 212/923-3700

This 67-acre park has eight miles of paths, and a garden of heather, a formal garden, and informal drifts of perennials and summer annuals against a background of hemlock, beech, chestnut and oak. This is an excellent garden of a type not often found in cities. The park is a good setting for a pleasant walk in the spring, especially along the paths that ultimately lead to the Cloister

Florists Who Can Make Flowers Speak for You

Some of the most articulate people in town allow flowers to speak for them, an old custom that hasn't lost its charm. Flowers have a large vocabulary. They can say thank you to a hostess, congratulations to a new mother, good luck in your new job, happy birthday, I share your loss, enjoy your new house, and, of course, I love you. Any of these florists will do you proud. They are among the best in the city.

Denis Flowers, **Hotel Intercontinental, 526 Lexington Avenue (48th–49th Streets) 212/355-1820 or 212/489-3647**
Fiori, **St. Regis Hotel, 2 East 55th Street (Fifth–Madison Avenues) 212/832-2430**
Zeze, **398 East 52nd Street (First Avenue) 212/753-7767**
Ronaldo Maia, **27 East Park Avenue (Lexington Avenue–67th Street) 212/288-1049**
Renny, **159 East 64th Street (Madison–Park Avenues) 212/288-7000**
Bloom, **16 West 21st Street (Fifth–Sixth Avenues) 212/620-5666**
The Potted Garden, **27 Bedford Street (6th–Downing Streets) 212/255-4797**
Elan Flowers, **148 Wooster Street (Prince–Spring Streets) 212/343-2426**

Gardens. Hours: sunrise to sunset daily. Free.

Garden of Enid, Institute of Physical Medicine and Rehabilitation
New York University,
400 East 34th Street
☎ 212/263-7300

This greenhouse has a selection of tropical and subtropical plants that are used by both the adult and child patients of the hospital as a form of therapy, either emotional or physical. Hours: 9 A.M. to 5:30 P.M. Monday to Friday, 1 to 5:30 weekends. Free admission.

New York Botanical Garden
200th Street at Southern Boulevard, Bronx
☎ 718/817-8700

This garden maintains 239 acres of landscaped grounds with 15,000 kinds of plants. The collection is so extensive that a visitor could spend years enjoying this wealth of plant material without having seen it all. The formal gardens are near the conservatory and the museum and include the lilac and magnolia collections. The Thompson Memorial Rock Garden covers more than three acres and contains 1,200 varieties. There are informal and formal flower beds and an outstanding rose garden. In the spring the liriodendron-lined roadway up to the museum is a joy. The last stand of hemlock forest in the city is here, along the Bronx River. The conservatory houses about 2,000 kinds of plants under two acres of glass. A palm house, a rain forest, a fern house, orchids, cycads, cacti, succulents, and seasonal displays are well worth seeing. May and June are good for the outdoor flowers, October and November for the chrysanthemums and other fall flowers. Garden hours: 10 A.M. to a half hour before sunset daily. The Conservatory is open from 10 A.M. to 4 P.M. Admission: free until noon, then $3 for adults, $2 for students and seniors. Charge for parking.

Queens Botanic Garden

43-50 Main Street, Flushing, Queens
☎ 718/886-3800

Here on twenty-six landscaped acres are a rose garden, an ericaceous garden, a fragrance garden, dwarf conifers, and an excellent collection of rhododendrons. There is as tulip display in the spring, roses in the summer, and chrysanthemums from mid-September to mid-November. A greenhouse also is on the grounds. Hours: 8 a.m. to dusk daily. Admission free.

Van Courtlandt Manor and Garden

Van Courtlandt Park, Broadway (near 242nd Street), Bronx
☎ 718/543-3344

On the grounds of this magnificent estate is a formal eighteenth-century garden reminiscent of its Dutch heritage.

Wave Hill

West 249th Street and Independence Avenue, Bronx
☎ 718/549-3200

This twenty-eight-acre garden estate includes wildflowers and a nature trail, a rose garden, herb garden, aquatic garden, palm court, and three greenhouses. Hours: 9 A.M. to 5 P.M. Thursdays through Sundays. Admission: adults $4, students and seniors $2, children under 12 free.

BROADWAY AND BEYOND

Give Your Regards to Broadway's Great Theaters

Nothing in the city is more wonderfully retro than the grand old theaters of Broadway. In the age of virtual reality, Broadway still works its magic. You can see for yourself by watching the faces of the children at *The Lion King,* or the faces of the adults at *Death of a Salesman.* Broadway theaters are also museums of sorts, repositories of the memories of past glories. An evening at the theater will be more enjoyable if you know something about the theater's history.

Ambassador
219 West 49th Street
(Broadway–Eighth Avenue)
Telecharge: ☎ 212/239-6200 or 800/432-2220

This theater has had a checkered career, switching from legitimate theater to motion-picture house to radio and television studios several times between 1935 and 1955, when the Shuberts repurchased the theater they had built and restored it to legitimacy. The Ambassador opened February 11, 1921, with *The Rose Girl,* and its hits included *Blossom Tie, The Great Gatsby, Springtime for Henry,* and *The Straw Hat Review* (which launched the careers of Imogene Coca, Alfred Drake, and Danny Kaye). Jumping ahead to the 1970s, hits here included *Ain't Supposed to Die a Natural Death,* Jim Dale in *Scapino,* Billy Dee Williams in *I Have a Dream,* and Estelle Parsons

in *Miss Margarida's Way.* The musical *Eubie* opened the 1980s, followed by Bob Fosse's smash hit *Dancin'.* Until recently, the Ambassador has housed revivals: *Dreamgirls, Ain't Misbehavin',* and Rex Harrison, Glynis Johns, and Stewart Granger in W. Somerset Maugham's *The Circle.* A recent offering here was *It Ain't Nothin' but the Blues.*

Brooks Atkinson
256 West 47th Street
(Broadway–Eighth Avenue)
☎ Ticketmaster: 212/307-4100

This theater, originally called the Mansfield, opened in 1926 with Marjorie Rambeau in *The Night Duel.* Antoinette Perry, for whom the Tonys were named, starred in *The Ladder.* The theater was a television playhouse from 1950 to 1960, and when it reopened as a legitimate theater, it was renamed in honor of Brooks Atkinson, the *New York Times* critic. Neil Simon's first Broadway play, *Come Blow Your Horn,* opened here. Ellen Burstyn and Charles Grodin starred in *Same Time, Next Year* and it ran more than three years. Jack Lemmon did *Tribute* here, and *Tally's Folly* with Judd Hirsch was awarded the Pulitzer Prize. Kevin Spacey received rave reviews here for his performance in the revival of Eugene O'Neill's *The Iceman Cometh.*

Barrymore
243 West 47th Street
(Broadway–Eighth Avenue)
☎ Telecharge: 212/239-6200

The Shubert brothers wanted to manage Ethel Barrymore so much that they promised to name a theater after her if she'd sign with them. She did, they did, and she opened this house in 1928 in *The Kingdom of God.* Fred Astaire went to Hollywood after starring in *The Gay Divorce* (filmed as *The Gay Divorcee*). Over the years the Barrymore has featured many great actresses. Lynn Fontanne in Noel Coward's *Design for Living; Pygmalion* with Gertrude Lawrence; Chekov's *Three Sisters* with Katherine Cornell, Judith Anderson, and Ruth Gordon. In the 1950s, Lilli Palmer joined Rex Harrison in *Bell, Book and Candle;* Jessica Tandy joined her husband, Hume Cronyn, in *The Fourposter;* Deborah Kerr was a hit in *Tea and Sympathy.* In the 1970s, Ingrid Bergman starred in Bernard Shaw's *Captain Brassbound's*

Conversion; Maggie Smith in *Lettice & Lovage*; and another fine British actress, Judi Dench, thrilled the audience in *Amy's View.*

Belasco
111 West 44th Street
(Seventh–Eighth Avenues)
☎ Telecharge: 212/239-6200

David Belasco began his theater career as a child actor in San Francisco and became the most important and influential producer on Broadway during the early twentieth century. His imaginative visual effects became part of contemporary stagecraft. He also was an eccentric who dressed in the garb of a priest and was a notorious womanizer. His theater, which opened in 1907, had an elevator stage, and an apartment for him. He produced *Madame Butterfly* and *Girl of the Golden West,* both of which were later adapted into operas by Giacomo Puccini. Mary Pickford, despite her great success in movies, believed that the high point of her career was a small part in Belasco's production of *The Warrens of Virginia.* After Belasco died in 1931, the theater presented such realistic drama as Sidney Kingsley's *Dead End* and Clifford Odets's *Golden Boy.* In the 1950s, NBC used the Belasco as a radio playhouse. After it returned to legitimate production, Josephine Hull starred in *The Solid Gold Cadillac,* and Noel Coward starred in his own play *Nude with Violin. The Rocky Horror Show* arrived in 1975, followed by Uta Hagen in *Hide and Seek,* then *Ain't Mis-behavin'* settled in for an extended run. The theater was dark for several years. After reopening, the Belasco housed the Lincoln Center production of *Ring Around the Moon*.

Booth
222 West 45th Street
(Broadway–Eighth Avenue)
☎ Telecharge: 212/239-6200

The Booth, at the north end of Shubert Alley, is regarded as the handsomest theater in New York. It was named for Edwin Booth, the greatest Shakespearean actor of his time, and has been the scene of many distinguished productions since it opened in 1913. Two Pulitzer Prize-winning plays had long runs here: Kaufman and Hart's *You Can't Take It with You* in 1936 and William Saroyan's *The Time of Your Life* in 1939. In 1950 Shirley Booth and Sidney Blackmer illuminated William Inge's *Come Back, Little Sheba*. Other important productions of that decade included *Visit to a Small Planet* and *Two for the Seesaw*. The '60s saw Mike Nichols direct Eli Wallach, Anne Jackson, and Alan Arkin in *Luv*, and saw James Patterson win a Tony in Harold Pinter's *The Birthday Party*. In the '70s two hits came to the Booth from the Public Theater: *That Championship Season*, which won the Pulitzer Prize, and *For Colored Girls Who Have Considered Suicide/When the Rainbow Is Enuf* . . . Another Tony winner was here in 1981: Bernard Pomerance's *The Elephant Man*. Other important productions of the '80s included *American Buffalo;*

Stephen Sondheim's *Sunday in the Park with George; Shirley Valentine;* and *Tru,* starring Robert Morse.

Broadhurst
235 West 44th Street
(Seventh–Eighth Avenues)
☎ Telecharge: 212/239-6200

This theater, with its array of balconies and fire escapes, was named for playwright George Broadhurst. It opened in 1917 with Bernard Shaw's *Misalliance,* and has been offering theatergoers memorable productions ever since. Bert Lahr introduced "You're the Cream in My Coffee" here in *Hold Everything*. In 1932 came Ben Hecht and Charles MacArthur's *Twentieth Century,* and another hit the next year, Sidney Kingsley's *Men in White*. Later that decade came *The Petrified Forest* with Humphrey Bogart in the tough-guy role that sent him on the way to Hollywood. Musical hits over the years included *The World of Suzie Wong, Fiorello, Cabaret*, Bob Fosse's *Dancin'*, and Peter Shaffer's smash hit *Amadeus*.

Broadway
1681 Broadway (52nd–53rd Streets)
☎ Telecharge: 212/239-6200

A number of theaters became movie houses over the years, but the Broadway went the other way. It opened as a movie house in 1924 and became a legitimate theater five years later. During the war years, this was the home of Irving Berlin's hit *This Is the Army, My Sister Eileen,* and *Carmen Jones*. Ethel Merman starred here in *Gypsy,* Barbra Streisand in *Funny*

Girl, Yul Brynner in *The King and I,*
Anthony Quinn in *Zorba,* and Patti
LuPone in *Evita.* At the turn of the
millennium, *Miss Saigon* started its
second decade at the Broadway.

Cort

138 West 48th Street
(Sixth–Seventh Avenues)
☎ Telecharge: 212/239-6200

The Cort has a reputation as a
lucky house. It opened on Decem-
ber 20, 1912, with Laurette Taylor
in *Peg o' My Heart,* which lasted
two years, a phenomenal run in
those days. Other early hits included
Victor Herbert's *The Wooing of
Princess Pat,* Eva Gallienne and
Basil Rathbone in *The Swan, Room
Service* with the Marx Brothers, and
Jose Ferrer in *Charley's Aunt.*
During World War II, popular
plays here included *The Eve of St.
Mark* and *A Bell for Adano* with
Fredric March. Post-war hits
included Katherine Cornell and
Cedric Hardwicke in *Antigone* and
Cornelia Otis Skinner in *Lady
Windermere's Fan.* Two Pulitzer
Prize winners arrived in the 1950s:
The Shrike and *The Diary of Anne
Frank.* The 1960s here included
Robert Redford in *Sunday in New
York* and Kirk Douglas in *One Flew
over the Cuckoo's Nest.* In the 1970s,
The Magic Show played here for
more than four years.

Ford Center for the Performing Arts

213-15 42nd Street
(Seventh–Eighth Avenues)
☎ Ticketmaster: 212/307-4550 or
800/223-7565

Two dilapidated but classic theaters
on 42nd Street, the 1903 Lyric and
the 1930 New Apollo, have been
combined into a single 1,830-seat
state-of-the-art complex. Happily,
much of the original ornate plaster
work was restored and remounted
for the debut production of
Ragtime, which has packed the
house for three years.

Gershwin

222 West 51st Street
(Sixth Avenue–Broadway)
☎ 212/307-4100

When this theater opened in 1972
as the Uris, it was the first new
Broadway theater since the 1920s.
Its second production, *Seesaw,* was
a hit and won Tonys for Michael
Bennett and Tommy Tune. In the
1970s, the Gershwin began
"Evenings With . . ." featuring such
performers as Sammy Davis Jr.,
Andy Williams, Anthony Newley,
and Nureyev and Friends. It presented George Gershwin's original
full score of *Porgy and Bess.* A big
hit here in 1979 was Stephen
Sondheim's *Sweeny Todd.* Over the
years, however, the theater has
been known for revivals, including
*The King and I, My Fair Lady,
Showboat,* and *Mame.* As 1999
drew to a close, the theater was
presenting yet another revival,
Cathy Rigby in *Peter Pan.*

Golden

252 West 45th Street
(Broadway–Eighth Avenue)
☎ Telecharge: 212/239-6200

This was the Theatre Masque when it opened in 1927. In 1933 the longest-running show of its time, *Tobacco Road,* was here. Other early successes included Cedric Hardwicke in *Shadow and Substance,* Philip Barry's *Here Come the Clowns,* and *Angel Street* starring Leo G. Carroll and Vincent Price. A number of comedies have enjoyed success here: *A Party with Comden and Green; An Evening with Mike Nichols and Elaine May; Beyond the Fringe* with Peter Cook, Dudley Moore, and Jonathan Miller; and Victor Borge's *Comedy in Music.* The Theatre Masque became the John Golden in 1937, but Golden sold it to the Shuberts a few years later. This became a movie house in the mid-'40s. After returning to theater it produced a number of distinguished plays: *The Gin Game* with Hume Cronyn and Jessica Tandy; *Crimes of the Heart; 'night Mother; Glengarry Glen Ross;* and the Tony-winning play *Side Man.*

Helen Hayes

240 West 44th Street
(Seventh–Eighth Avenues)
☎ Ticketmaster: 212/944-9450

This is the second theater named for the late great actress. The first was demolished to make room for the Marriott Marquis. This one was the Little Theatre, built in 1912 to present intimate dramas. When it opened in 1912, it had only 299 seats but was later enlarged to 499.

A 1929 hit was *Let Us Be Gay.* Edward G. Robinson starred in *Mr. Samuel.* Cedric Hardwicke made his American debut here. In the Depression, the theater was first a conference center, then a television studio. It became a theater again in 1963 and a year later presented Paul Newman and Joanne Woodward in *Baby Want a Kiss.* It again became a TV studio in 1974, and over the next ten years the Merv Griffin and David Frost shows originated here. The latest theatrical reincarnation began in 1974, and the house began to have hits: Milan Stitt's *The Runner Stumbles, Gemini,* and *Torch Song Trilogy.*

Imperial

249 West 45th Street
(Seventh–Eighth Avenues)
☎ Telecharge: 212/239-6200

Younger theatergoers may think this theater was built expressly to house *Les Miserables,* in its thirteenth year in 1999, but it has been host to hit musicals since it opened in 1923. *Oh Kay!* by the brothers Gershwin was a success in 1926 with Gertrude Lawrence, as was Victor Herbert's *Babes in Toyland.* Moss Hart teamed with Cole Porter to score with *Jubilee,* and Rodgers and Hart had a winner with *On Your Toes.* Beginning in the 1940s a string of hits starred the irrepressible Ethel Merman— *Louisiana Purchase, Annie Get Your Gun,* and *Call Me Madam.* Then came the phenomenal *Fiddler on the Roof,* starring Zero Mostel, which ran for 3,272 performances. Before *Les Miserables* settled in for

Times Square at night

a marathon run, New Yorkers enjoyed the hit *Jerome Robbins' Broadway.*

Longacre
220 West 48th Street
(Broadway–Eighth Avenue)
Telecharge: 212/239-6200

Times Square was once called Longacre Square, and producer H. H. Frazee borrowed the name when he built this theater in 1913. Miriam Hopkins starred in the musical hit *Cobra.* Joan Bennett appeared with her matinee-idol father, Richard Bennett, in *Jarne-gan,* an expose of Hollywood. The Group Theatre used the Longacre for three plays by Clifford Odets: *Waiting for Lefty, Till the Day I Die,* and *Paradise Lost.* From 1944 to 1953, the Longacre was a radio and television studio. Later four Julie Harris vehicles were staged here: *Mademoiselle Colombe, The Lark, Little Moon of Alban,* and *The Belle of Amherst.* Other memorable plays here included Zero Mostel in *Rhinoceros,* Rita Moreno and Jack Weston in *The Ritz,* and John Gielgud and Ralph Richardson in Harold Pinter's *No Man's Land.*

Lunt-Fontanne
Broadway and 48th Street
☎ Telecharge: 212/239-6200

Charles Dillingham built this theater to house his productions and named it the Globe. It opened with *The Old Town* on January 10, 1910. He spared no expense to make it the handsomest theater, and he entertained stars and backers in lavish apartments in the upper stories. During the Depression he lost the theater and it became a movie house until the late 1950s. Then it was extensively refurbished, the entrance moved to 48th Street, and renamed to honor America's most distinguished acting couple, Alfred Lunt and his wife, Lynn Fontanne. The theater reopened on May 5, 1958, with *The Visit*. In late 1959, *The Sound of Music* opened, starring Mary Martin, and logged 1,443 performances. Other productions included Richard Burton in *Hamlet*, Robert Preston in *Ben Franklin in Paris*, and Hal Linden in *The Rothchilds*. Most recently the theater was home to *Beauty and the Beast*, starring Andrea McCardle.

Lyceum
149 West 45th Street
(Sixth Avenue–Broadway)
☎ Telecharge: 212/239-6200

Producer Daniel Frohman was the first to come north from 23rd Street and build in the present theater district, but he put his theater on the wrong side of Broadway. Some say this is the most beautiful theater in the city, with its columns, mansard roof, and luxurious nineteenth-century interior

appointments. It opened in 1903 and some of its early productions included Leslie Howard in *Berkeley Square* and Ina Claire and Walter Slezak in *When We Are Married*. In the 1940s came Kaufman and Hart's *George Washington Slept Here*, *The Late George Apley*, and Judy Holliday and Paul Douglas in *Born Yesterday*. In the 1950s were Odet's *The Country Girl* and John Osborne's explosive *Look Back in Anger*. The Lyceum presented the Tony winners *Borstal Boy* and *Mornings at Seven*, Constance Cummings in *Wings*, and Whoopi Goldberg's one-woman show.

Majestic
247 West 44th Street
(Broadway–Eighth Avenue)
☎ Telecharge: 212/239-6200

This is one of the largest and most elegant theaters, with a large, illuminated dome in the ceiling and an elevated orchestra floor. The Majestic is admirably suited to musical comedies. It opened in 1927, and its early productions included Gertrude Lawrence in *The International Review* and Sigmund Romberg's *Nina Rosa*. *Carousel* was a hit here in 1945, and for a decade the theater was practically a Rodgers and Hammerstein house, with *Allegro*, *South Pacific*, and *Me and Juliet*. Shirley Booth starred in *By the Beautiful Sea*, Ezio Pinza in *Fanny*, and Robert Preston in *The Music Man*. Later came *The Wiz*, winner of seven Tonys, and Liza Minnelli's *The Act*. Then *42nd Street* settled in for a six-year run, only to be followed by a super hit, Andrew Lloyd Webber's *Phantom of the Opera,* which as of late 1999 had been playing at the Majestic for 12 years.

Martin Beck

302 West 45th Street
(Eighth–Ninth Avenues)
☎ Telecharge: 212/239-6200

Martin Beck, head of the old Orpheum vaudeville circuit, built this theater west of Eighth Avenue despite predictions that theatergoers wouldn't cross the avenue. The theater opened in late 1924 with a production of *Madame Pompadour* and remained in the Beck family until 1966, although the Theatre Guild used it for several years. The Lunts appeared here in *Reunion in Vienna,* Katherine Cornell in *The Barretts of Wimpole Street,* and Basil Rathbone, Edith Evans, and Orson Welles in *Romeo and Juliet.* Later Paul Lukas starred in Lillian Hellman's *Watch on the Rhine,* Tennessee Williams's *The Rose Tattoo,* Arthur Miller's *The Crucible,* and *Sweet Bird of Youth,* costarring Paul Newman and Geraldine Page. *Bye Bye Birdie* was a hit here, and so was Elizabeth Taylor in her Broadway debut in Hellman's *The Little Foxes.*

Marquis

1535 Broadway (46th Street)
☎ Ticketmaster: 212/307-4100

The Marriott Marquis, a 47-story hotel fronting Times Square, cost a quarter of a billion dollars and three Broadway theaters to build. It replaced the Helen Hayes, the Bijou, and the Morosco. But despite opposition, the hotel was

completed in 1985 and it contained a new theater, the Marquis. The opening production, *Me and My Girl,* was a hit and proceeded to run more than three years. As the millennium neared, Bernadette Peters was displaying her marksmanship at the Marquis in the hit revival of Irving Berlin's *Annie Get Your Gun.*

Minskoff

200 West 45th Street
(west of Broadway)
☎ Ticketmaster: 212/307-4100

The old Astor Hotel was theater district landmark for more than fifty years. Many actors stayed there, and the Hunt Room served as their private club. In 1968 the Astor was torn down and replaced with a fifty-five-story office tower that included this theater, named after Jerry Minskoff, the developer. It has backstage space second only to the Metropolitan Opera. It opened in 1972 with a smash hit, the revival of *Irene,* starring Debbie Reynolds. In the 1980s, *Pirates of Penzance* was here for awhile, as was the revival of *Sweet Charity.* A late 1999 offering at the Minskoff was the musical-theater adaptation of the motion picture *Saturday Night Fever.*

Music Box

239 West 45th Street
(Broadway–Eighth Avenue)
☎ Telecharge: 212/239-6200

Irving Berlin and his producer, Sam H. Harris, built this theater to house the composer's *Music Box Revues,* opening with the *Music Box*

Ten Great Broadway Musicals about New York

A Chorus Line
Fiorello!
42nd Street
George M!
Guys and Dolls
Hello, Dolly!
How to Succeed in Business Without Really Trying
Knickerbocker Holiday
West Side Story
Wonderful Town

Revue of 1921. Berlin's revues continued through 1925, followed by the Pulitzer Prize winner *Of Thee I Sing.* Curiously, since then the Music Box has had more hit plays than musicals: Tennessee Williams's *Summer and Smoke,* William Inge's *Picnic* and *Bus Stop,* Harold Pinter's *The Homecoming.* Later came *Sleuth* and *Deathtrap,* both big hits, *Agnes of God,* and *Les Liaisons Dangereuses.*

Neil Simon

250 West 52nd Street
(Broadway–Eighth Avenue)
☎ Theater Direct: 800/334-8457 or Ticketmaster: 212/307-4100

Renamed in 1983 to honor Broadway's most successful playwright, this was the Alvin, which opened in 1927 with a smash hit: The Gershwins' *Funny Face,* starring

Fred and Adele Astaire. Ethel Merman made her Broadway debut here in another Gershwin hit, *Girl Crazy,* and starred here in the Cole Porter hit *Anything Goes!* with Jimmy Durante and Bob Hope. George M. Cohan returned to the stage here to star as FDR in *I'd Rather Be Right.* During the Depression, CBS used it as a radio playhouse. In the 1940s, Gertrude Lawrence and Danny Kaye sizzled in *Lady in the Dark.* Merman was back in Porter's *Something for the Boys,* and the decade closed with one of the theater's biggest hits, Henry Fonda in *Mister Roberts.* Other hits through the years included Zero Mostel in *A Funny Thing Happened on the Way to the Forum* and Stephen Sondheim's *Company.* Since then the theater has showcased mostly Neil Simon comedies, including *Brighton Beach Memoirs* and *Biloxi Blues.* In the late 1990s, the Neil Simon was the home of the long-running *The Scarlet Pimpernel.*

Nederlander

208 West 41st
(Seventh–Eighth Avenues)
☎ Ticketmaster: 212/307-4100

Built in 1921 and called the National Theater, this theater has had hits alternating with long dark periods. The first hit was *Grand Hotel;* other early successes included *Ethan Frome,* starring Pauline Lord, Ruth Gordon, and Raymond Massey; Gertrude Lawrence and Noel Coward in *Tonight at 8:30;* Orson Welles and the Mercury Theatre Company in *Julius Caesar;*

and Tallulah Bankhead in *The Little Foxes*. Hits of the 1940s included Ethel Barrymore in *The Corn is Green*, Maurice Evans and Judith Anderson in *Macbeth*, John Gielgud in *Medea*, and Lilli Palmer and Cedric Hardwicke in *Caesar and Cleopatra*. The 1950s saw Paul Muni and Ed Begley in *Inherit the Wind*. Showman Billy Rose bought the theater in 1959, refurbished it, and gave it his name. In the 1960s, Edward Albee's *Who's Afraid of Virginia Woolf?* threatened to run forever. James and Joseph Nederlander bought the theater in the 1970s and renamed it the Trafalgar. After two hits—*Whose Life Is It Anyway?* and *Betrayal*—the theater was renamed again, this time in honor of the late David Tobias Nederlander. Another long run came in the late 1990s, the Tony-winner *Rent*.

New Amsterdam Theatre
214 West 42nd Street
(Seventh–Eighth Avenues)
☎ Ticketmaster: 212/307-4100

The great showman Florenz Ziegfeld built this magnificent theater in 1903. Ziegfeld devised and perfected the American revue spectacle, based on the *Follies Bergeres*. He opened his *Follies of 1907*, the first of an annual series that continued until 1931, and made his name synonymous with extravagant theatrical production. The *Follies* featured a chorus line of beautiful young women, all personally chosen to "glorify the American girl." Ziegfeld died in 1932 and his theater lay fallow until Disney

acquired it in the 1990s. Disney spent $36 million restoring and refurbishing the elaborate art nouveau interior to its original grandeur and installing a high-tech sound system. This is now the home of Disney theatrical productions, including the megahit *The Lion King*.

New Victory Theatre
209 West 42nd Street
(Seventh–Eighth Avenues)
☎ Ticketmaster: 212/307-4100

Built in 1900 by Oscar Hammerstein, this is the city's oldest active theater. Its handsome interior had a large dome with plaster angels around its rim. Two years later, though, producer David Belasco bought the theater and completely renovated it to his taste. When 42nd Street began to go downhill, the theater ran the gamut from burlesque shows to second-run movies. In 1955 the New Victory was the first to be restored on the "New 42nd Street." Much of the original interior has been restored, the dome is intact, and the grant Venetian staircase was reconstructed. The theater now features family-oriented productions—vaudeville, puppet shows, ballet, and circuses.

Eugene O'Neill
250 West 49th Street
(Broadway–Eighth Avenue)
☎ Ticketmaster: 212/307-4100

When it opened in 1925, this theater was named the Forrest in honor of Edwin Forrest, the great nineteenth-century actor. For a while it was the Coronet before it became the Eugene O'Neill in 1959 to honor America's greatest playwright. Despite the name, O'Neill's plays never seem to be performed here. It has had its share of outstanding productions, though, which include the premier of *Tobacco Road*, Arthur Miller's *All My Sons*, and Lillian Hellman's *The Children's Hour*. In the 1970s, the theater was purchased by Neil Simon and a number of his comedies opened here: *Last of the Red Hot Lovers, The Prisoner of Second Avenue, The Good Doctor, God's Favorite, California Suite*, and *I Ought to Be in Pictures*. The 1990s saw *M. Butterfly*, and revival of Arthur Miller's *Death of a Salesman*, starring Brian Dennehy.

Palace

1564 Broadway (47th Street)
☎ Ticketmaster: 212/307-4100

The Palace was once known as the "Valhalla of Vaudeville." It was the showcase of the Keith-Albee circuit, which booked vaudeville acts throughout the country, until vaudeville died in the early 1930s. Everyone who was anyone performed here: W. C. Fields, Houdini, Jack Benny, Fred Astaire, Will Rogers, Sophie Tucker, even Sarah Bernhardt. After three decades as a movie house, it became a theater in 1966, and its first production, *Sweet Charity* with Gwen Verdon, was a hit. Other hits followed, including Sondheim's *Applause*, which won a Tony for Lauren Bacall; *La Cage aux Folles*, which ran for four years; and,

more recently, the Disney production of *Beauty and the Beast*.

Plymouth

236 West 45th Street
(Broadway–Eighth Avenue)
☎ Telecharge: 212/239-6200

Arthur Hopkins, a producer known for his good taste, built this theater in 1917, and it has built a reputation for housing important plays. One of the first productions here was *Redemption*, staring John Barrymore. His brother, Lionel, starred in *The Jest* two years later. *Abe Lincoln in Illinois*, starring Raymond Massey, won the Pulitzer Prize, as did Thornton Wilder's *The Skin of Our Teeth*, with Fredric March, Tallulah Bankhead, Florence Eldridge, and Montgomery Clift. The 1950s saw *Don Juan in Hell* with Charles Laughton, Agnes Moorehead, Charles Boyer, and Cedric Hardwicke. Other plays in that period included *Dial M for Murder, Tiger at the Gates, Romanoff and Juliet*, and *The Marriage-Go-Round*. In the '50s came *Irma la Douce, Tchin-Tchin*, Lillian Hellman's *My Mother, My Father*, and Alec Guinness in *Dylan*. Later there was some comic relief with Art Carney and Walter Matthau in *The Odd Couple*, and Maureen Stapleton and George C. Scott in *Plaza Suite*. Peter Shaffer's *Equus*, one of the important plays of the 1970s, was a hit here, and much later came long-running *Jekyll & Hyde*.

Richard Rodgers
226 West 46th Street
(Broadway–Eighth Avenue)
☎ Ticketmaster: 212/307-4100

Originally called the 46th Street Theater, this theater opened on Christmas Eve, 1925, with a musical and has housed mostly musicals ever since. In 1927, Zelma O'Neill made the varsity drag a popular dance in *Good News*. Two years later *Follow Thru* featured two promising newcomers, Eleanor Powell and Jack Haley. Ginger Rogers was a hit in *Top Speed,* and Fanny Brice and George Jessel had a winner in *Sweet and Low*. In 1945, Ethel Merman was a big hit in *Anything Goes*. Two more Merman hits also were here: *Du Barry Was a Lady* and *Panama Hattie*. The theater was also home to three Gwen Verdon hits: *Damn Yankees, New Girl in Town,* and *Redhead*. Other hits included *Finian's Rainbow, Guys and Dolls,* and the Pulitzer Prize winner *How to Succeed in Business Without Really Trying*. Remember *The Best Little Whorehouse in Texas*? It was here, and so was *Do I Hear a Waltz?, I Do! I Do!,* the revival of *No, No, Nanette,* and *Nine*. In 1990 the name of the theater was changed to honor the late composer Richard Rodgers.

Royale
141 West 42nd Street
(Broadway–Eighth Avenue)
☎ Telecharge: 212/239-6200

This theater opened in 1927 and got its first hit the next season with *Diamond Lil,* starring Mae West,

Ten Great Broadway Plays about New York

Angels in America
Arsenic and Old Lace
Barefoot in the Park
Dead End
Detective Story
The Iceman Cometh
Life with Father
Tru
Two for the Seesaw
(And, of course, all of Neil Simon's comedies)

who had previously been fined $500 and given ten days in the workhouse for her risqué performance in *Sex*. The 1930s saw Claude Rains in *They Shall Not Die,* Paul Muni in *Counselor-at-Law,* and Sir John Gielgud in *The Importance of Being Earnest*. Producer John Golden leased the theater and changed its name to the Golden before it was taken over by CBS in 1936 and used as radio theater until 1940. Returning to stage theater with its original name, the Royale in the '50s saw Gielgud return with the young Richard Burton in Christopher Fry's *The Lady's Not for Burning,* Eartha Kitt and Alice Ghostley in *New Faces of 1952,* and Laurence Olivier in both *The Entertainer* and *Becket*. In 1961, Tennessee Williams's *The Night of the Iguana* opened here to acclaim.

The Ed Sullivan Theater

This landmark theater, built in 1927, has housed vaudeville, a music hall, stage shows, and a nightclub, then became the home of the Fred Allen radio show. From 1948 to 1971 it was the home of *The Ed Sullivan Show*, and here American television audiences got their first look at Elvis Presley, the Beatles, and Rudolf Nureyev. It is now the home of *Late Show with David Letterman*. 1697 Broadway (53rd–54th Streets)

The 1963 Pulitzer Prize play, Frank Gilroy's *The Subject Was Roses*, enjoyed a long run, as did *Cactus Flower* with Lauren Bacall. Many theatergoers remember the Royale as the home of *Grease*, which opened off Broadway to tepid reviews, later settling in here to set a new Broadway record of 3,388 performances. Later hits here included *Joseph and the Amazing Technicolor Dreamcoat, Speed the Plow*, and *Lend Me a Tenor*.

St. James
246 West 44th Street
(Broadway–Eighth Avenue)
☎ Telecharge: 212/239-6200

Originally this was the Erlanger, the showcase of Abraham Erlanger's Theatrical Syndicate. It opened September 26, 1927, with George M. Cohan's *The Merry*

Malones. In 1932 new owners renamed it for the St. James Theatre in London. Some of the early productions included Tyrone Power in *Diplomacy* and Minnie Maddern Fiske in *Ladies of the Jury*. In the 1930s Walter Slezak appeared in Sigmund Romberg's *Fine Wine*, and the Orson Welles production of *Native Son* starred Canada Lee. A smash hit, Rodgers and Hammerstein's *Oklahoma!*, arrived in 1943 and stayed five years. Other hits here were *Where's Charley?* (1948), *The King and I* (1951), and *The Pajama Game* (1954). One of the theater's great hits arrived on January 16, 1964. *Hello Dolly!* starred first Carol Channing, then Ginger Rogers, Pearl Bailey, Martha Raye, Betty Grable, and Ethel Merman. It played here for six years.

Shubert
225 West 44th Street
(Seventh–Eighth Avenues)
☎ Telecharge: 212/239-6200

This is the flagship theater of the Shubert organization, and its executive offices are above the theater in what was once Lee Shubert's apartment. Although it opened in 1913 with a production of *Hamlet*, the Shubert has housed mostly musicals. In the 1920s, the Dolly Sisters highlighted the *Greenwich Village Follies*, and Texas Guinan was a hit in *Padlocks of 1927*. A memorable play (which became a memorable movie) came in 1939: *The Philadelphia Story*, starring Katharine Hepburn with Van Heflin, Joseph Cotton, and Shirley

Booth. Several delightful Rodgers and Hart musicals were here in that decade: *Babes in Arms, I Married an Angel, Higher and Higher,* and *By Jupiter.* Later offerings included Lerner and Loewe's *Paint Your Wagon* and Cole Porter's *Can-Can.* Celeste Holm starred in *Bloomer Girl,* Barbra Streisand made her Broadway debut in *I Can Get It for You Wholesale,* and Glynis Johns was a hit in Stephen Sondheim's *A Little Night Music.* Then came *A Chorus Line,* which won every award in sight and played 6,137 performances. At the millennium, *Chicago,* winner of six Tonys, was about to enter its fourth year here.

Studio 54
254 West 54th Street
(Broadway–Eighth Avenue)
☎ Telecharge: 212/239-6200

In the swinging 1970s, this was the place in the city to let it all hang out—if the bulky bouncer recognized you or liked your looks and let down the velvet rope. The music was loud, cocaine was plentiful, and there were celebrities galore at play. It all came to an end when the owners were charged with tax evasion and sent to jail. After standing empty for a number of years, Studio 54 was refurbished and made its debut as a theater. In 1999 it was hosting a revival of the hit musical *Cabaret.*

Sullivan Street Playhouse

This 153-seat theater is the home to the longest-running production in American history, *The Fantasticks,* by Tom Jones and Harvey Schmidt. The play opened here the night of May 3, 1960, and the end isn't in sight yet. The show has played in more than 2,000 cities and towns in this country, and in 65 foreign countries. In 1988 an American company toured Japan, winding up in Tokyo, where it alternated with the Japanese company that had been presenting *The Fantasticks* for 18 years. Jerry Orbach was in the original production, and over the years the cast has included Anna Maria Alberghetti, Elliott Gould, Bert Lahr, Liza Minnelli, Tom Poston, John Carradine, Richard Chamberlain, Howard Keel, John Raitt, and John Wood. If you'd invested $100 in the original production, you'd be a millionaire and then some. The city has named this block of Sullivan Street "Fantasticks Lane." If you live in New York and haven't seen *The Fantasticks,* you should be ashamed. 181 Sullivan Street (West Houston–Bleecker Streets) 212/674-3838

Times Square

In 1904, anticipating the move of *The New York Times* to the midtown area, the mayor and the board of aldermen changed the name of Longacre Square to Times Square. The area is bounded by Broadway, Seventh Avenue, and West 42nd and West 47th Streets. Today it is the heart of the Theater District and the site of some of the most spectacular electric advertising signs ever created. The Times Tower was built over the city's largest subway station, and to make room for the newspaper's presses the basement had to be blasted out of solid rock fifty-five feet down. The presses rolled on

January 2, 1905, after the new year had been welcomed with the dropping of a lighted ball down the flagpole on the roof. The celebration has been repeated every year since.

At the north end of Times Square is Duffy Square, bounded by Seventh Avenue and Broadway, and West 46th and West 47th Streets. Father Francis P. Duffy, chaplain of the Fighting 69th regiment in World War I, served as pastor of the nearby Holy Cross

Times Square

Church and is honored in this triangle with a life-size sculpture. Nearby is a sculpture of George M. Cohan, the actor/writer/producer who wrote "Give My Regards to Broadway" and hundreds of other popular songs.

Virginia
245 West 52nd Street
(Broadway–Eighth Avenue)
☎ Telecharge: 212/239-6200

This theater was built for and named for the Theatre Guild. It opened in April 1925 with a production of *Caesar and Cleopatra,* and President Calvin Coolidge threw a switch in the White House to light the stage. For a number of reasons the theater was unpopular with actors and audiences, and it was leased as a radio playhouse in 1933. The American National Theatre and Academy (ANTA) bought the house in 1950 and renamed it after itself. It was renamed the Virginia in 1981. Productions in that period included

Twentieth Century with Jose Ferrer and Gloria Swanson, a revival of Thornton Wilder's *The Skin of Our Teeth* with Mary Martin and Helen Hayes. The theater was the home of the long-running *A Man for All Seasons* and later the Pulitzer Prize–winning *No Place to be Somebody*. Other important plays here included Jimmy Stewart and Helen Hayes in a revival of *Harvey*, Tom Stoppard's *Night and Day*, the musical *David Copperfield*, and Larry Gelbart's *City of Angels*.

Walter Kerr

219 West 48th Street
(Broadway–Eighth Avenue)
☎ Telecharge: 212/239-6200

This theater has had more lives than a cat. Opened by the Shuberts as the Ritz in 1921, it became a showcase for the great ladies of the stage; Ina Claire, Katharine Cornell, Lynn Fontanne, Claudette Colbert, Helen Hayes, Miriam Hopkins, and Bette Davis all starred here. In the 1930s came Ruth Draper, Mildred Natwick, Ilka Chase, Peggy Conklin, Jessica Tandy, and Sybil Thorndike. In 1939 the Ritz became a CBS studio and later an NBC television studio. The city acquired it in the 1960s and renamed it the RFK Center, but soon it fell into disuse. Jujamcyn Theatres acquired and renovated,

but what followed was a string of forgettable productions. After a few years the site became a movie theater. In 1983 Jujamcyn again renovated the theater and renamed it for newspaper critic Walter Kerr. August Wilson's Pulitzer Prize–winning *The Piano Lesson* had its Broadway run here.

Winter Garden

1634 Broadway (50th Street)
☎ Telecharge: 212/239-6200

From the start, this handsome theater was lucky for singers and dancers. Al Jolson opened the theater on March 20, 1911, in a twin bill, *Bow Sing* and *La Belle Paree*. Fred Astaire and his sister Adele had their first triumph here in 1912, *Over the Top*. Billie Burke was the star of the 1934 *Ziegfeld Follies*, and Ray Bolger joined Bert Lahr in *Life Begins at 8:40*. A later edition of the *Ziegfeld Follies* featured Fanny Brice and Josephine Baker. In the 1950s, this was the home of Tammy Grimes's *The Unsinkable Molly Brown*, Leonard Bernstein's *West Side Story*, Barbra Streisand's *Funny Girl*, and Angela Lansbury's *Mame*. Grimes and Jerry Orbach were sensations in *42nd Street*, and to top it all off came *Cats*, the longest-running show in Broadway history.

Off Broadway

Off Broadway is a recent term for alternate theater, and by the 1920s the city had a vigorous alternate theater centered in Greenwich Village. Three of the best-known groups were the Neighborhood Playhouse, the Washington Square Players, and the Provincetown Players, and the plays of Eugene O'Neill were first produced here. Alternate theater struggled through the Depression and the war years but blossomed again in the 1950s and 1960s.

One would think that the term Off Broadway refers to location, but it really has to do with money. Actors Equity and the other theatrical unions have agreed to a lower pay scale for smaller theaters. Broadway theaters are big, and many seat 1,500 and up. Off Broadway theaters seat 300 or less and are scattered all over the city. Because it's much less expensive to produce plays Off Broadway, you'll usually see more adventurous theater there, and you'll pay less: Tickets cost from $15 to $45. An important part of the Off Broadway scene is production companies, groups that put on a series of plays each season. Many companies are associated with a particular theater while others rent theaters when they have a play ready for the public. These companies and theaters are among the best known and most respected:

Atlantic Theater Company
336 West 20th Street
(Eighth–Ninth Avenues)
☎ 212/645-1242
This group was an offshoot of the acting workshop of playwright David Mamet and actor William H.

Macy. It has produced 17 plays, including Mamet's *Edmond* and the premieres of Howard Korder's *Boy's Life*, Craig Lucas's *Missing Persons*, and the American premiere of Martin McDonagh's *The Beauty Queen of Leenane*.

La MaMa E.T.C.
74A East 4th Street
(Bowery–Second Avenue)
☎ 212/475-7710

This theater was a force in the Off Broadway movement practically from the beginning. Ellen Stewart opened La MaMa (Mama is her nickname) in 1962. Harvey Fierstein's *Torch Song Trilogy* premiered here. Over the years it has garnered more than fifty Obie (Off Broadway) awards, and it's a fixture in the city's dramatic life.

Manhattan Theater Club
City Center, 131 West 55th Street
(Sixth–Seventh Avenues)
☎ 212/581-1212

The club's two theaters, now located in the basement of City Center, offer four plays each year by both established and new playwrights. Among its premieres are Simon Gray's *The Rear Guard,* Athol Fugard's *The Blood Knot,* and Joe Orton's *What the Butler Saw.* The Fats Waller musical *Ain't Misbehavin'* was developed here.

New York Theatre Workshop
79 East 4th Street
(Second Avenue–Bowery)
☎ 212/460-5475

Founded 30 years ago, this company produces new plays using young directors. Besides premiering works by such directors as David Rabe *(A Question of Mercy)* and Caryl Churchill *(Mad Forest),* the workshop first presented Jonathan Larson's musical *Rent,* which went on to win the Pulitzer Prize.

Playwright's Horizons
416 West 42nd Street
(Ninth–Tenth Avenues)
☎ 212/564-1235

This company has premiered more than 300 plays, including *The Substance of Fire, The Heidi Chronicles, Driving Miss Daisy,* and musicals, including *Sunday in the Park with George* and *March of the Falsettos.*

The Public Theater
425 Lafayette Street
(Astor Place–East 4th Street)
☎ 212/539-8500

Founded by the late Joseph Papp, this Astor Place landmark has consistently presented some of the most interesting theater in the city. It is dedicated to presenting the work of new American playwrights and performers, and also presents new explorations of Shakespeare and other classics. The building houses five stages and a cabaret space. George C. Wolfe now runs the Public and is responsible for *Bring in 'da Noise, Bring in 'da Funk,* and the New York production of Tony Kushner's *Angels in America.*

The Vineyard Theater
108 East 15th Street
(Union Square East)
☎ 212/353-3874

This subscription theater in Union Square presents new plays and musicals, and occasionally tries to revitalize works that have failed in other arenas. It has recently been on a roll; the hits include Paula Vogel's *How I Learned to Drive* and Edward Albee's *Three Tall Women.*

Off-Off Broadway

Off-Off Broadway is another modern term for alternate theater. Off-Off Broadway theaters have fewer than 100 seats and are allowed to employ actors who are not members of Actors Equity, the theatrical union. As a result, Off-Off Broadway productions cost much less than Off Broadway productions. And Off-Off Broadway is where writers, directors, and actors have the opportunity to experiment. Some Off-Off Broadway theaters present traditional contemporary plays. Most Off-Off Broadway theaters are downtown (the Village, SoHo, East Village, and TriBeCa), although many do not have their own theaters. Tickets cost from $10 to $25. Some of the best known theaters include:

Adobe Theater Company
453 West 16th Street
(Ninth–Tenth Avenues)
☎ 212/352-0441

More than 25 shows have been presented by this non-profit company in the past eight years. Their off-the-wall works appeal to young, hip audiences that appreciate the pop-culture references. Recent stagings include *Notions in Motions,* a juicy update of Pirandello; *The Handless Maiden,* a modern fable; and *Duet!,* a romance for cynics.

Bouwerie Lane Theatre
330 Bowery (Bond Street)
☎ 212/677-0060

The old cast-iron German Exchange Bank is the home of the Jean Cocteau Repertory Company, which is devoted to producing the classics in repertory. Recent presentations include Joe Orton's *What the Butler Saw,* Tom Stoppard's *Rough Crossing,* and Seamus Heaney's *The Cure at Troy.*

En Garde Arts
☎ 212/279-1461

This company presents what is called site-specific theater throughout the city. It produced *Stonewall 25* on the scene of the original riot, *J.P. Saves the Nation* right in the middle of Wall Street, *The Trojan Women* at a graffiti-covered abandoned amphitheater on the East River, Tyne Daly in *Mystery School* in a synagogue, and Fiona Shaw's rendition of T. S. Eliot's *The Waste Land* at the Liberty Theater while it was being renovated.

Drama Dept.

☎ 212/541-8299

This is a new company which had two early hits—Carter Beane's *As Bees in Honey Drown* and a revival of Lardner and Kaufman's *June Moon*. The company is backed by Hollywood money and has first-rate writers, directors, and actors. It hires various theaters for its productions.

Irish Repertory Theatre

132 West 22nd Street
(Sixth–Seventh Avenues)
☎ 212/727-2737

Not surprisingly, this Chelsea company is dedicated to performing works from both classic and contemporary Irish playwrights. Notable productions include Frank McCourt's *The Irish and How They Got That Way* and Hugh Leonard's *Da.*

The Kitchen

512 West 19th Street
(Tenth–Eleventh Avenues)
☎ 212/255-5793

For more than 25 years, this small, experimental theater has been presenting an eclectic repertoire of theater, music, dance, video, and performance art. Laurie Anderson, David Byrne, and Cindy Sherman began their careers here.

The Performing Garage

122 Wooster Street
(Broome–Grand Streets)
☎ 212/477-5288

This is the home of the talented Wooster Group, whose members include Richard Foreman, Willem Dafoe, Elizabeth LeCompte, and

Spalding Gray. Gray developed his well-known dialogues here, including *Swimming to Cambodia*. Dafoe once played the lead in O'Neill's *The Hairy Ape* and a blackface version of *The Emperor Jones*.

Second Stage Theatre

2162 Broadway (76th Street)
☎ 212/787-3392

Created for American plays that didn't receive the reception they deserved, Second Stage also produces the works of new American playwrights. It staged the premiere of Lanford Wilson's *Sympathetic Magic* and the revival of his *Lemon Ski*. It premiered Tina Howe's *Painting Churches* and *Coastal Disturbances*, and David Mamet's *The Woods.*

Signature Theatre Company

555 West 42nd Street
(Tenth–Eleventh Avenues)
☎ 212/244-7529

This award-winning company focuses on the works of a single playwright in residence. The playwrights have included Edward Albee, Sam Shepard, Arthur Miller, and Horton Foote, whose *The Young Man from Atlanta* originated here and went on to win the Pulitzer Prize.

Theater for the New City

155 First Avenue (9th–10th Streets)
☎ 212/254-1109

The Living Theater Group, which is in residence here, usually stages hard-hitting political drama. There are four theaters in the building, which is the home of the Out on the Edge Festival of Lesbian and Gay Theater.

TKTS and Tickets

To be a savvy New Yorker, one must know how to procure good theater tickets on demand at the lowest possible price. Here are some tips:

The **Theater Development Fund** maintains a ticket booth at Duffy Square, north of Times Square. Tickets to Broadway shows (and some Off Broadway shows) are sold on the day of the show at half price plus a $2.50-per-ticket service charge. A sign tells what is on sale. No credit cards or personal checks accepted.

A better selection is sometimes available close to curtain time, when producers release house seats, and during bad weather, when fewer people venture out. Another good time to buy is on Mondays and Tuesdays, when most theaters alternate closing. Tickets go on sale at 10 A.M. for matinees, 3 P.M. for evening performances. Duffy Square, West 46th and West 47th Streets, Seventh Avenue and Broadway. ☎ 212-768-1818

Another TKTS booth is in the Financial District at 2 World Trade Center (Liberty–Vesey Streets). ☎ 212-768-1818

Another way to get bargain tickets is to send $14 to the **Theater Development Fund,** 1501 Broadway, 21st floor, New York, NY 10036, and you'll be sent ticket vouchers for really inexpensive shows. TDF subsidizes some Broadway and Off Broadway productions, and buys large blocks of discounted seats that are then turned over to the subscribers.

Hit Show Club

Mail a self-addressed, stamped envelope to the Hit Show Club, which manufactures and distributes "twofer" coupons redeemable at the box office for a third off nearly any Broadway show. ☎ For information: 212/581-4211. Ask about special non-member prices on Broadway.

Standing Room

Many large theaters sell standing-room tickets, at $10 to $15, but only if a show is nearly sold out. Check with the box office. Once in, look for empty seats; they are yours for the taking.

High "5" Tickets

Some theaters offer discounts to junior high or high school students. The price is $5 for two tickets, Monday to Thursday; $5 for one ticket, Friday to Sunday. ☎ For details: 212/445-8587.

Tickets by Phone

If you want the convenience of

ordering tickets by phone, check in the alphabetical listings for ticket services in the *New York Times,* or phone either ☎ Telecharge, 212/239-6200 (outside New York, 800/432-7250), or Ticketmaster, 212/307-4100 (outside New York, 800/755-4000). Your tickets will be held for you at the theater's box office.

Previews

Few Broadway plays preview out of town these days, and it's much easier to get good seats to a preview than to a performance after the show has opened—assuming the reviews are good. You risk seeing a flop in the making, or a hit before it has everything in final form. Occasionally previews offer exceptional bargains. Some shows preview with a progressive ticket-price incentive. For the first preview, all seats are, say, $20; the second preview, $25, and so on. Shows that have no big-name stars often use such gimmicks to lure preview audiences in the hope that good word-of-mouth will build audiences. Some people are uncomfortable at previews; the show hasn't been reviewed and they don't know how to react. Personally, we like to form our own opinion and see if the critics agree.

Thursday night specials

Around 8 on Thursday night, a theater's house tickets (good seats held by the producer in case celebrities or other VIPs show up) are released to be sold to the public. If you're lucky, you'll have great seats for Saturday night at regular prices.

Must tickets

The Actor's Fund has four house seats to every Broadway show that are available to anyone who is willing to pay double the face value of the ticket and calls within 48 hours prior to performance. Half the ticket price is tax deductible as a contribution to the Actor's Fund. ☎ 212/221-7300, ext. 133

Buy at the box office and save

If possible, buy tickets at the theater box office. You'll be treated better, you can see on the seating plan where your seats are, and you'll save money. Telecharge, Ticketmaster, and similar services charge a healthy handling fee.

Free tickets for children

More and more Broadway shows offer free tickets for children to adults who pay full price. ☎ 212/302-4111 (out of town: 888/411-BWAY)

AWAY FOR THE WEEKEND

Ten Great Getaways

New Yorkers have been getting away from the city since New York became a city. During the colonial era, people would go to what now is Greenwich Village. As the city expanded northward, they would visit the Bronx. With the coming of public transportation, they would head for the beaches of Long Island or the Jersey shore. Later, garment workers found relief from the city's heat and noise in the Catskills. Now as then, the city blahs can be cured by getting away for the weekend. Here are some tried-and-true places where you'll find some lovely retro pleasures.

West Point, New York

In the fall, when the air is crisp and the leaves are a riot of color, you can drive up to West Point for a football game in Michie Stadium. It's an unforgettable experience. The Corps of Cadets parades in the late morning, everyone tailgates in the parking lot for lunch, and the game is great fun; when Army scores, a cannon is fired, and a cheerleader rides the mule mascot around the field. A good place to stay is the Hotel Thayer at the Thayer entrance gate. When it was built in 1926, it was named for an early superintendent, Sylvanus Thayer, who set the academy's rigorous standards.

You can spend Sunday leisurely exploring the campus. One-hour bus tours leave from the Visitor Center (for times, ☎ 914/446-4724).

During the Revolution a huge chain was placed across the Hudson here to prevent British ships from using the river. Overlooking the Hudson is the Battle Monument, on which is inscribed the names of the 2,230 Union officers killed in the Civil War. The beautiful Cadet Chapel is on a hill overlooking the campus. Be sure to leave time to browse in the West Point museum, which is filled with memorabilia of American wars, from the Revolution to Vietnam.

West Point is about 60 miles north of the city. To drive there, cross the George Washington or Tappan Zee Bridge, go north to the end of the Palisades Parkway, and at the Bear Mountain traffic circle, take Route 9W north to Route 218 to the academy. For information, phone the academy: 914/938-2638. For reservations at the Hotel Thayer, phone 800/247-5047.

The Hamptons, Long Island
Unless you have money to burn, visit the Hamptons after Labor Day. The traffic is light, the crowds gone, the prices lower, and the natives friendlier. In contrast to a summer weekend, you'll have the place to yourself. You can walk on the beach, rent a sailboat, and play golf or tennis. If you don't feel that energetic, you can visit the art galleries and museums or shop. You may enjoy taking the Montauk Highway to the tip of the island, visit the lighthouse, and go out on a cruise boat from Montauk Harbor.

Let's say you're staying at the lovely Victorian inn called The Hedges in East Hampton. It offers a restaurant (James Lang Cafe), a complimentary continental breakfast, privileges for tennis and a nearby nine-hole golf course, and it's a half-mile from the beach. **The Hedges (516/324-7100)** is a good base for exploring East Hampton, which was settled in 1648 and was farm country until it became a fashionable resort around the time of the Civil War.

Stop by the **"Home Sweet Home" House**, the childhood home of John Howard Payne, who wrote the haunting song **(516/324-0713)**. The adjacent **Historic Mulford Farm** is a living-history farm museum, which the kids will love **(516/324-6850)**. Don't miss the Guild Hall museum, which features regional art

exhibits. And at the Guild Hall is the 400-seat **John Drew Theater**, which features plays, films, concerts, lectures, and children's performances. **(516/324-4050 or 0806)**. Note: Most attractions are open only on weekends during September.

If you drive, take the Long Island Expressway (I-495) to exit 70 (Route 111 South) then follow Route 27 East into the Hamptons. The Long Island Rail Road provides daily service from Penn Station to the Hamptons. 718/217-5477 for timetable and fare information.

Saratoga Springs, New York
Enjoy Victorian architecture? Racing? Symphonic music? If you answer yes to any of these, come here in August. They all await your pleasure. "Society, sport and sin," one writer explained, were the ingredients that made this town America's premier resort in the 1800s. Some came to this town for the waters, believed to cure all sorts of ailments. Others came to drink champagne and gamble. Saratoga Springs reached its apex right after the Civil War, attracting the likes of Diamond Jim Brady, Boss Tweed, and Commodore Vanderbilt. Broadway, the main street, was lined with great hotels.

Three millionaires built the **Saratoga** racetrack and sponsored the first running of the Travers, America's oldest racing event. The racetrack, unchanged over the years, offers top-caliber thoroughbred racing during August **(514/584-6200)**. The **National Museum of Racing (518/584-0400)**, across the street from the race-track, is well worth a visit. Saratoga is also a showplace of Victorian architecture, and 900 of its houses are on the National Register of Historic Places. You can taste the waters that made Saratoga famous in Congress Park, where the information center is located. In the park is the 1870 Canfield Casino, now a museum with Victoriana and gambling parapher-nalia. The celebrated Philadelphia Orchestra plays at the **Saratoga Per-forming Arts Center (518/587-3330)**. A fine place to stay is the **Gideon Putnam Hotel**, adjacent to the Performing Arts Center in Sara-toga Spa State Park. If you come in August, be sure to reserve a room well in advance **(518/584-3000)**.

If you drive, cross the George Washington or Tappan Zee Bridge and take the Palisades Parkway to the New York Thruway (I-87) north to Albany, then continue 32 miles north to Saratoga Springs.

Brandywine Valley, Pennsylvania
The southeastern corner of Pennsylvania has more than its share of interesting places to visit. The best known is **Longwood Gardens**, which is one of the great public gardens of the world. It was created by Pierre S. du Pont, who purchased the land in 1906. It con-sists of 300 landscaped acres, 700 acres of meadow and woodland, and four acres of glass conservato-ries. More than 14,000 types of plants are grown here. At the Main Fountain Garden, water is sprayed 130 feet in the air. The displays in the

glass conservatories are changed seasonally, and there are events for visitors year-round **(610/388-6741)**. In 1777, during the Revolution, Chadds Ford, five miles northeast of Longwood, was the scene of the bloody Battle of the Brandywine, now commemorated by the fifty-acre Brandywine Battlefield State Park. It was here Washington failed to stop the British force marching on Philadelphia. Washington's headquarters and the house used by Lafayette both may be visited, and the story of the bat-tle is told in exhibits in the visitor center **(610/459-3342)**.

Chadds Ford is also the birth-place and home of artist Andrew Wyeth, and the Brandywine River Museum, just south of town, dis-plays the work of the entire Wyeth family and other important artists who settled in the valley. The museum, a converted old gristmill on the river, houses works by Howard Pyle, the first American illustrator of note, N. C. Wyeth, father of Andrew and a famed illustrator in his own right, Max-field Parrish, and Frank Schoon-over. One of its galleries is devoted to the works of Andrew Wyeth and his family members, includ-ing his son Jamie **(610/459-3342)**. An excellent place to stay is the comfortable **Fairville** in Menden-hall, which is on Route 1 going west from Chadds Ford, then south on Route 52 to Mendenhall. The inn is a half-mile past Mendenhall on the left **(610/388-5900)**.

To reach the Brandywine Valley from New York, take the New Jersey Turnpike south to exit 2 (Route 322) west over the Commodore Barry Bridge into Pennsylvania and continue to Route 452. Take 452 north to Route 1 and continue along Route 1 to the various sites.

Cape May, New Jersey

Unlike some of its noisy neighbors, Cape May is a genteel haven and architectural treasure, which befits its position as the oldest seaside resort in the country. In the mid-1800s, summering here was the height of fashion. Cape May had 57 hotels and was known as the "Resort of Presidents"—Buchanan, Pierce, Grant, Harrison, and Lincoln all vacationed here, along with such notables as Horace Greeley and John Wanamaker. Cape May was eclipsed by the rise of Atlantic City, but was rediscovered in the 1900s and was extensively restored. Today practically the entire town of more than 600 Victorian summer cottages, which are painted in the subtle colors and pastels of the time, is a National Historic Landmark.

You'll enjoy Cape May's four miles of beaches, 1¼-mile paved promenade, and trolley. It's fun to walk the shores of Delaware Bay, hunting for "Cape May diamonds," which are actually pure quartz, rounded by the waves. Some fascinating tours are offered by the **Mid-Atlantic Center for the Arts:** Mansions by Gaslight is a three-hour tour visiting four Victorian landmarks, and an Ocean Walk tells about marine life and buried

treasure **(609/884-6404)**. If you have the time, the 16-mile, 76-minute ferry ride across the bay to Lewes (pronounced Lewis), Delaware, is a joy on a sunny day **(302/645-6313)**. Seafood lovers rhapsodize about dinner at Axelson's Blue Claw. And there are nearly a dozen B&Bs, all in lovely old Victorian houses, including the Abbey, a Gothic-style building with a sixty-foot tower that was built in 1869 **(609/884-4506)**.

From New York, take the Garden State Parkway to the end, bear left and take the Cape May Canal Bridge, which leads onto Lafayette Street and into Cape May.

Connecticut River Valley

Near the mouth of the Connecticut River is the town of Essex, where in 1775 the first American warship, the *Oliver Cromwell,* was built. Not much has happened since, but Essex has morphed into the kind of New England town you see in movies, and it's an ideal place to forget the problems of the city. Essex offers visitors a number of diversions. The Valley Railroad is a twelve-mile scenic steam train excursion along the river to Chester, where you can opt to return on a riverboat cruise **(203/767-0310)**. Visit the Gillette Castle, an architectural folly built in 1917 by William Gillette, who made millions for years playing the role of Sherlock Holmes. The castle is ugly, no doubt about that, and comes complete with a number of fake doors and secret hiding places. Gillette amused his guests by taking them around the grounds on a miniature railroad. The view across the river is marvelous. **Gillette Castle State Park 860/526-2336**

The treasure around here is the **Goodspeed Opera House** in nearby East Haddam. The opera house is a Victorian theater built on the river's edge by a local shipbuilder and banker in 1876. Restored in the 1960s, it is now the home of the American Musical Theatre. Three musicals are presented each season, some old and some new. Among the shows developed here are *Man of La Mancha, Shenandoah,* and *Annie.* It is a gem of a theater with exceptional acoustics, and to sip champagne on the terrace at intermission and to see the lights twinkling on the river is a rare treat. Make your reservations well in advance **(203/873-8668)**.

Another treat is the **Griswold Inn** in Essex, which has been greeting guests since 1776. It's furnished with antiques, and the dining room has a great collection of marine paintings, prints, and artifacts. In addition to good food, the dining room serves up banjo concerts and a jazz pianist on weekends **(203/767-1776)**.

To drive to Essex, take the New England Thruway (I-95) to Route 9 (exit 70) and go north.

Rhinebeck, New York

If you love old airplanes, you must visit the **Old Rhinebeck Aerodrome** and see its world-famous collection of vintage planes, dating from the early 1900s to the late 1930s. On weekends from May to October, pilots reenact World War I dogfights, and, for a fee, will take you up for a flight in an open-cockpit biplane **(914/758-8610)**.

If you love famous houses, there are two just south on Route 9 in Hyde Park. The most famous is **Springwood,** the birthplace and lifelong home of Franklin D. Roosevelt. The interior is furnished just as it was when Roosevelt died. The graves of Roosevelt and his wife, Eleanor, are in the Rose Garden **(914/229-9115)**. The most beautiful is the **Vanderbilt Mansion,** a 1898 Beaux Arts palace designed by McKim, Mead & White for Frederick W. Vanderbilt. The grounds offer superb views up and down the Hudson **(914/229-9115)**. Another beauty is the **Mills Mansion,** a Greek Revival mansion that was remodeled and enlarged in 1895 by McKim, Mead, and White into an 84-room, neoclassical country residence for Ogden Mills. It is furnished in a blend of the styles of Louis XIV, Louis XV, and Louis XVI, with tapestries, art objects, marble fireplaces, and gilded plasterwork **(914/889-8851)**.

If you love classic French cuisine, dine at **The Escoffier Restaurant**, which is run by students at the Culinary Institute in Hyde Park. The prix fixe dinner is especially recommended. Be sure to make your reservation well in advance, however; it is very popular **(914/471-6608)**. And if you love great inns, stay at the historic **Beekman Arms**, which has been delighting guests since 1766, and may well be the oldest inn in continuous operation in the country. It's furnished with antiques, of course. The **Beekman 1766 Tavern** has a good buffet breakfast, and at dinner the cedar plank salmon is highly recommended **(914/876-7077** for the inn, **914/871-1776** for the tavern).

From New York, take the Taconic State Parkway and turn left at the Rhinebeck exit. Hyde Park is about five miles south of Rhinebeck on Route 9.

Mystic, Connecticut

From the early 1800s to the Civil War, Mystic was one of the most important shipbuilding sites in the country. Yards here built coastal sloops, fishing vessels, and magnificent clipper ships. Mystic's *Andrew Jackson* set the world speed record in the 1850s for sailing around Cape Horn to San Francisco.

Mystic Seaport is a re-creation of the glory days here. It consists of more than sixty buildings on seventeen acres, and is a "living" museum where people practice traditional maritime crafts. Among the many exhibits are a ropewalk, rigging loft, hoop shop, printing press, drugstore, bank, cooperage, smithy, and sail loft. The premier attraction, however, is the 1841 sailing ship the *Charles W. Morgan*, which made thirty-seven voyages from the South Seas to the Arctic, earning $1.4 million for her New Bedford owners. The 111-foot ship could carry 2,700 barrels of whale oil. Something is going on every day at the seaport: seasonal trips aboard rowboats, steamboats, and sailboats; sea chantey concerts; and workshops in shipbuilding **(860/572-5955)**.

A short drive from Mystic is Groton, a name synonymous with submarines. At the USS *Nautilus* Memorial is the world's first nuclear-powered vessel. The submarine was launched in 1954, and in 1958 she sailed under a polar ice cap from the Pacific to the Atlantic. You can see her operations deck, torpedo room, living quarters, and dining areas. Practically next door is the **Submarine Force Library and Museum** with material covering the history of submarines from the Revolution to the present. Among the exhibits are ship models, working periscopes, and a control room. On the grounds are Japanese midget submarines and an early research submarine, the *Explorer* **(203/449-3558)**.

The Inn at Mystic is an excellent place to stay, and the whirlpool in the heated pool will help you relax after a long day of sightseeing **(800/237-2415)**.

From New York to Mystic, take I-95 north to exit 90, pick up Route 27 and continue to the seaport. To reach the sub base, take I-95 north to exit 86.

Cooperstown, New York

Baseball made Cooperstown famous, but a lot of other things made it interesting. It became a popular summer resort, but it never developed industrially; as a result, the village is about the same as it was in the early days. It was founded in 1786 by James Fenimore Cooper's father, Judge William Cooper, and the town was the center of the author's "Leatherstocking Tales." The town is on the south end of ninety-mile-long Otsego Lake, which is called Glimmerglass in Cooper's stories. **Fenimore House** is a museum that exhibits Cooper memorabilia and has an outstanding collection of American folk art **(607/547-2533)**.

A must-see is the **Farmers' Museum and Village Crossroads**, which is a re-creation of an early nineteenth-century village with a dozen commercial and residential buildings. Among the artifacts is the Cardiff Giant, unearthed in 1869 on a farm in Cardiff, New York. The ten-foot-tall figure, thought to be a petrified prehistoric man, was exhibited widely but it turned out to be a hoax **(607/547-2533)**.

Any baseball fan can spend hours happily in the **National Baseball Hall of Fame**, which is filled with the stuff of dreams. The Babe Ruth room has his bat and locker. You'll see Rickey Henderson's shoes from the season he set the stolen-base record. Interactive video screens let you choose which player you want to see in action. One exhibit shows the evolution of the catcher's mask; another has the original scores of popular songs about baseball. One room is dedicated to baseball movies **(607/547-7200)**.

A nice, convenient place to stay is the **Inn at Cooperstown**, the former annex to the Fenimore Hotel, built in 1874, furnished with Victorian pieces, and still handsome **(607/647-5756)**.

To drive to Cooperstown, take the New York Thruway (I-87) to Albany, then go west on I-88 to Route 20, continuing west on Route 80 south. Continue along the west shore of Otsego Lake to Cooperstown.

Pennsylvania Dutch Country

The plain and fancy co-exist in Lancaster County, some sixty-five miles west of Philadelphia. This is Pennsylvania Dutch country, home to the Plain people (the Amish, Mennonite, and Brethren), descendants of German and Swiss immigrants. Visitors come here to see the Old Order Amish, who cling to the old ways. They shun such amenities as electricity and cars, preferring gas lamps and horse-drawn carriages. Ironically, while they have turned their back on the modern world, they have attracted its attention.

A good way to orient yourself is to take a tour. **Amish Country Tours**, between Bird-in-Hand and Intercourse **(717/768-8400)**, offers a variety of bus and minivan tours. If you yearn for a buggy ride over the scenic back roads, make arrangements with **Ed's Buggy Rides (717/687-0360)**. The **Historic Lancaster Walking Tour** is a ninety-minute stroll through the charming old city, conducted by guides in period costumes **(717/392-1776)**.

You'll have a wide choice of sites to see. **Amish Farm and House** in Lancaster will show you traditional Amish life **(717/394-6185)**. A former Mennonite meeting place, The

Hans Herr House, five miles south of Lancaster, is the oldest house in the county. Dating from 1719, it is an outstanding example of medieval German styles. When you're saturated with local culture, you might enjoy a scenic nine-mile ride in a turn-of-the-century train to Paradise and back. Phone the **Strasburg Rail Road** for details **(717/687-7522)**. Also in Strasburg is the well-stocked **Railroad Museum of Pennsylvania (717/687-8628)**, and the **Toy Train Museum (717/687-7911)**.

   The Village Inn of Bird-in-Hand is a Victorian-style country inn with down-filled bedding and cable TV in its eleven guest rooms. The inn gives guests a free two-hour tour of the area **(717/293-8369)**. The nearby **Bird-in-Hand Family Restaurant** is a good place to sample regional specialties **(717/768-8266)**.

From New York, take the New Jersey Turnpike south to exit 6, which will connect with the Pennsylvania Turnpike. Take the turnpike to exit 22, and follow scenic Route 23 south to Lancaster. Lancaster is approximately 65 miles west of Philadelphia.

INDEX

Numbers in *italics* indicate
photographs.

Aaron Faber, 161
Abbey, the, 203
Abraham Erlanger's
    Theatrical Syndicate, 188
Academy (bookstore), 154
Academy of Arts and Letters,
    30
Academy of Music, 127
Actor's Fund, 198
Actors Equity, 192, 194
Adams, Abigail, 64
Adams, F. P., 52
Adams, John, 64, 68, 69
Adams, Michael Henry, 118
Admiral Farragut Monument
    (Saint-Gaudens), 16
Adobe Theater Company, 194
Adventures on a Shoestring,
    86
Advertising Club, 18
Affair to Remember, An, 71
Afro-Cuban Jazz Orchestra,
    119
AIDS Care Center of New
    York Hospital–Cornell
    Medical Center, 160
Alexander and Bonin, 147
Algonquin, The, 52, 98–99,
    112
Alienist, The (Carr), 155
All About Eve, 150
All Night Walking Tours, 136
Allen, John, 140
Allen, Woody, 119, 122
Alliance Francaise, 152
alternate theater, 192–95
Altman, B., 15–16
Alvin Ailey American Dance
    Center, 143
Alvin theater, 184
Amato Opera, The, 127
Ambassador theater, 176
Ambrose, 9, 58
American Ballet Theatre, 143
American Museum–Hayden
    Planetarium, 61
American Museum of the
    Moving Image, 62–63
American Museum of
    Natural History, 61, 88,
    88
American Musical Theatre,
    204
American National Theatre
    and Academy, 190
American Notes (Dickens), 84
American Numismatic
    Society, 30
American Opera Projects,
    127–28

American Revolution, 8, 12,
    22, 32, 34, 36, 38, 64, 65,
    67, 69, 200, 202
American Wristwatches—Five
    Decades of Style and
    Design (Faber and
    Unger), 161
Amish Country Tours, 206
Amish Farm and House, 206
Anderson, Sherwood, 13
Andre Emmerich, 147
Andrew Jackson, 205
Angelo and Maxie's, 102
Angels in America, 187
Annex Antiques Fair and Flea
    Market, 162
Ansonia Brass and Copper,
    49
Ansonia Hotel, 49
Apollo, The, 116
Applause (bookstore), 156
Appleton, William Henry, 66
arch at Grand Army Plaza, 36
architectural styles
    art deco, 45, 56
    Beaux Arts, 45, 49, 204
    cast-iron, 12, 194
    Dutch, 68
    Dutch Colonial, 65, 67
    Edwardian, 55, 56
    Edwardian-French, 47
    English, 68
    Federal, 10, 15, 48, 65
    French Gothic, 43
    French Renaissance, 48
    French Second Empire, 36
    Georgian, 10, 92
    German Renaissance, 48
    Gothic, 36, 43, 77
    Gothic Revival, 64, 69
    Greek Revival, 10, 15, 42,
        43, 63, 204
    Italianate, 36
    medieval German, 207
    neo-Byzantine, 43
    neo-Gothic, 48
    Queen, 36
    Queen Anne, 24
    Renaissance, 18, 20, 59
    Romanesque, 24, 44, 48
    Second Empire, 16
    Victorian, 10, 36, 201, 202,
        203
archy and mehitabel (Marquis),
    155
Argosy, 155
Arsenal, 130
Arsenic and Old Lace, 187
art deco architecture, 45, 56
art galleries, contemporary,
    147–48
Arthur Murray dance studios,
    143
Arthur's Tavern, 118

Asia de Cuba, 103
Asia Society, 149
Asian-American Festival Day,
    164
Astor, John Jacob, 55, 66
Astor, William B., 30
Astor, William Waldorf, 20
Astor family, 12, 20
Astor Hotel, 183
Astor library, 50
Astor Place District, 12–13
Astoria hotel, 20
Astoria Studios, 15, 33, 63
Atlantic Attic, 165
Atlantic City, 203
Atlantic Theater Company,
    193
auctions, 158–59
Audubon, John James, 30, 62
Audubon Bar and Grill, 116
Audubon Heights Museum
    Group, 30
Audubon Society, 148
Audubon Terrace, 30
Aureole, 101
Austen, Alice, 69
Austen (Alice) House, 69
Axelson's Blue Claw, 203

B. Altman's, 20
Bacall, Lauren, 48
Baker, Jean-Claude, 99
Baker, Josephine, 99
Ball Park Lanes, 135
Ballet Hispanico School of
    Dance, 144
Bank of New York, 38
Bar and Books, 103
Barbetta, 99
Barefoot in the Park, 187
Bargemusic, 124
Barnard College, 29
Barnum, P. T., 35
Barrymore, Ethel, 106, 177
Barrymore, John, 15
Barrymore theater, 177
bars, 105–107
Bartos (Celeste) Forum at the
    New York Public Library,
    126
Bartow, Robert, 67
Bartow-Pell Mansion and
    Gardens, 67, 170
baseball, 3, 38, 205, 206
Bastille Day, 164
Battery City, 169
Battery Park, 37, 83, 170
Battle of the Brandywine, 202
Battle of Long Island, 34, 67
Battle Monument, 200
Beasley, 39
Beatles, The, 47
Beaux Arts architecture, 45,
    49, 204